At Issue

| Slavery Today

Other Books in the At Issue Series:

At Issue

DISCARDED

Slavery Today

Ronald D. Lankford, Jr., Book Editor

GREENHAVEN PRESS
A part of Gale, Cengage Learning

GALE
CENGAGE Learning™

Detroit • New York • San Francisco • New Haven, Conn • Waterville, Maine • London

Christine Nasso, *Publisher*
Elizabeth Des Chenes, *Managing Editor*

© 2010 Greenhaven Press, a part of Gale, Cengage Learning.

Gale and Greenhaven Press are registered trademarks used herein under license.

For more information, contact:
Greenhaven Press
27500 Drake Rd.
Farmington Hills, MI 48331-3535
Or you can visit our Internet site at gale.cengage.com

For product information and technology assistance, contact us at

Gale Customer Support, 1-800-877-4253
For permission to use material from this text or product, submit all requests online at www.cengage.com/permissions

Further permissions questions can be emailed to permissionrequest@cengage.com

Articles in Greenhaven Press anthologies are often edited for length to meet page requirements. In addition, original titles of these works are changed to clearly present the main thesis and to explicitly indicate the author's opinion. Every effort is made to ensure that Greenhaven Press accurately reflects the original intent of the authors. Every effort has been made to trace the owners of copyrighted material.

Cover image © Images.com/Corbis.

LIBRARY OF CONGRESS CATALOGING-IN-PUBLICATION DATA

Slavery today / Ronald D. Lankford, Jr., book editor.
   p. cm. -- (At issue)
Includes bibliographical references and index.
ISBN 978-0-7377-4440-8 (hbk.)
ISBN 978-0-7377-4441-5 (pbk.)
   1. Slavery--United States--History--21st century. 2. Human trafficking--United States. 3. Slave labor--United States. I. Lankford, Ronald D., 1962-
   HT867.S53 2009
   306.3'6209730905--dc22

                                                      2009020987

Printed in the United States of America
2 3 4 5 6 7 13 12 11 10 09

Contents

Introduction

Many people are surprised to learn that even though slavery is illegal in most countries, it is a rampant socioeconomic problem that exists on a global scale. Kevin Bales of Free the Slaves has estimated that there are 27 million slaves today, more than at any time in history. People are also surprised to learn that slavery continues to exist even in countries like the United States. The Central Intelligence Agency (CIA) estimates that 50,000 women and children are brought into the United States every year to work as sex slaves, and that a number of others are forced to work in garment factories, as agricultural workers, and as domestic laborers.

Traditionally, the practice of human bondage was referred to as chattel slavery. In chattel slavery, slaves and any of their offspring were the property of the owner. In this relationship, the master was basically free to assign any work to the slave, to sell or trade the slave, or even to abuse the slave physically or sexually. Frequently, chattel slavery was racially based as was the case in the United States in the eighteenth and nineteenth centuries. Traditional chattel slavery is seldom practiced in the contemporary world. Instead, contemporary slavery takes a number of forms.

Understanding these multiple forms of slavery helps to avoid a great deal of confusion. Trafficking may be a type of slavery, for instance, but it is far from the only type. Likewise, the various manifestations of slavery reveal how prevalent this human rights problem is. It is easy, perhaps, to imagine someone being enslaved as a sweatshop worker in a poverty-stricken distant country, but shocking to learn that a domestic worker in one's own neighborhood might be a slave. The major types of contemporary slavery include:

- Bonded labor or debt bondage—bonded labor is the most common type of slavery today. In essence, bonded labor begins when men and women are asked to work to pay off a personal debt or the debt of a family member. Because the worker is paid so little, however, it becomes difficult if not impossible for the laborer to pay back his or her debt. In some cases, workers are controlled by physical and sexual threats and violence. Poverty is perhaps the biggest reason for bonded labor, leading to various arrangements to pay off debt. For instance, a poor family that inherits a debt may allow their children to become bonded laborers to help pay back the money owed.

- Forced domestic labor—many workers in poor regions migrate to wealthier countries to work as nannies, cooks, housekeepers, gardeners, and personal servants. However, a number of these workers are exploited and some are enslaved. The employers who exploit domestic workers often take advantage of them by holding their passports or threatening to deport the workers if they happen to be illegal aliens. In addition, the workers may become entrapped simply because they do not know the native language and are therefore unable to explain their situation. As with bonded laborers, domestic workers are sometimes physically and sexually abused. Enslaved domestic workers are also difficult to detect because for all intents and purposes they perform the same tasks as other domestic workers.

- Forced prostitution—often when commentators speak of human trafficking in relation to slavery, they are speaking of prostitution. As with domestic workers, many women and children are promised employment in a new country. Once they arrive, however, they are entrapped in sexual slavery. As with forced domestic labor, it is often difficult for authorities to distinguish between women who have chosen to work as prostitutes and those who have been forced into prostitution. A number of young women are also sold into sexual slavery in countries such as India and Pakistan. Other practices, such as bride kidnapping or servile marriages, are sometimes listed as types of forced prostitution. In both cases, women and children are forced to marry against their consent.

• Child soldiers—it has been documented that children as young as nine have been abducted and forced to serve in the military. A number of these child soldiers are trained to serve as cooks and spies; many even take part in active combat. While it is less frequently documented, young girls have also been abducted into the military, and they are oftentimes subjected to sexual abuse. It was estimated that during the Ethiopian civil war that ended in 1991, 25% of the participants were girls. In 2007, a CNN report projected that there were some 250,000 child soldiers throughout the world, though determining how many of these children have been recruited against their will is impossible to establish.

Perhaps the greatest challenge that anti-slavery advocates and aid workers face in seeking to draw international attention to the exploitation of human beings is overcoming deeply ingrained cultural attitudes toward slavery and clarifying the scope of the problem. Indeed, it is often difficult to ascertain whether a person has chosen to work in a particular field like prostitution or domestic labor or whether they have been forced into the occupation. There is also a fine line between workers who are paid, though perhaps paid very little, and those who are enslaved and not paid at all. In many sweatshops, for instance, it is difficult to distinguish among willing, exploited, and enslaved workers. Critics have also pointed out that the prison system in a number of countries provides labor either free of charge or at a highly reduced rate. While few would argue that slavery no longer exists, many disagree about what exactly constitutes slavery.

Even if slavery today is defined in the most conservative manner, it continues to be a controversial human rights problem both in developed and undeveloped countries. The future challenge for government authorities, law enforcement officials, and citizens is twofold. First, there is a need to increase public awareness of the problem in order to help to identify those who are being held against their will. Second, new economic and social policies need to be implemented in order to eliminate poverty and many of the other reasons slavery thrives around the world. While no solution promises to bring a swift or even a complete end to slavery today, the fact that more people are beginning to recognize the scope of the problem will serve as a first step toward grappling with the human dimension of the issue.

1

Slavery in the United States Is a Serious Problem

Janet Gilmore

Janet Gilmore works in media relations at the University of California, Berkeley.

Most people believe that the institution of slavery is part of the historical past, but slavery continues today, even in the United States. A report by the organization Free the Slaves found that forced labor is practiced in 90 American cities. While forced labor exists in many parts of the United States, states with large immigrant populations are the worst offenders. Forced laborers are frequently abused and held against their will, but the public is generally unaware of these practices. By raising public awareness about the practice of forced labor it can be brought into the open and eradicated.

A new report on forced labor in the United States reveals in disturbing detail how individuals in communities across the country are forced through threats or violence to work in deplorable conditions for little or no pay.

The report, "Hidden Slaves: Forced Labor in the United States," describes for the first time the nature and scope of modern-day slavery in America.

Released during a news conference in Washington, D.C., today (Thursday, Sept. 23 [2004]), the report was conducted

Janet Gilmore, "Modern Slavery Thriving in the U.S.," *UC Berkeley Media Relations*, September 23, 2004. Reproduced by permission.

by researchers from the University of California, Berkeley's Human Rights Center and the Washington, D.C.-based anti-slavery group Free the Slaves.

Forced labor occurs in at least 90 cities across the United States, the researchers found, and at any given time, 10,000 or more people are forced to toil in sweat shops, clean homes, labor on farms, or work as prostitutes or strippers.

A Contemporary Problem

"The most shocking aspect of this report is that modern-day slavery still exists," said Laurel Fletcher, a researcher at the Human Rights Center and professor at UC Berkeley's law school. "Slavery is a problem the public thinks we solved long ago, but, in fact, it's alive and well. It has simply taken on a new form."

And the form of slavery will continue to change, said Kevin Bales, president of Free the Slaves. "It is important to remember that slavery is a crime and that criminals are always looking for new ways to exploit people."

Victims of forced labor are trafficked into the United States from at least 38 different countries, with China, Mexico, and Vietnam topping the list.

Cases documented in the report include a Berkeley, Calif., businessman who enslaved young girls and women for sex and to work in his restaurant; a Florida employer who threatened violence to force hundreds of Mexican and Guatemalan workers to harvest fruit; and two couples in Washington, D.C., who brought Cameroonian teenagers to the United States with the promise of a better education and then forced them to work 14 hours a day as domestic servants, without pay and under the threat of deportation.

Among the report's major findings:

- While forced labor exists across the United States, reported cases are concentrated in states with large immigrant communities, including California, Florida, New York, and Texas.

- Victims of forced labor are trafficked into the United States from at least 38 different countries, with China, Mexico, and Vietnam topping the list. Some are born in the United States and later held captive.

- Forced labor occurs in poorly regulated industries with a high demand for cheap labor—sweatshops, restaurants, and hotels, in addition to agriculture and domestic work. A lack of official monitoring in these areas means unscrupulous employers and criminal networks can gain complete control over workers.

- Forty-six percent of those trapped in forced labor in America are found in prostitution and sex services, the study estimates. Another 27 percent are domestic workers, and one in 10 works in agriculture. These victims are spread across the economy—sweatshop/factory work makes up 5 percent; restaurant and hotel work [make] up 4 percent. Sexual exploitation of children represents 3 percent.

Captives Held By Force

The new study documents how modern slavery operates in the United States. Perpetrators use a range of crimes—fraud, coercion, physical and psychological violence—to hold their victims captive. They confiscate passports and threaten to turn their captives over to the authorities if they refuse to obey. In some cases, perpetrators and their associates threaten or physically attack the families of victims in their home countries.

"Victims may be verbally abused, beaten or sexually assaulted by their captors," said Eric Stover, director of the Human Rights Center and faculty member at UC Berkeley's School of Public Health. "These repeated attacks, especially against children and teenagers, can result in serious physical and psychological trauma."

Even if victims can escape, they often fear leaving because they do not speak English, are unfamiliar with U.S. currency, and are unsure of how to use local transport.

In a strange land, victims can grow dependent on their captors, if only to survive.

Lack of Public Awareness

According to Bales, "The lack of public awareness of slavery in America makes this report very important. People are literally living next door to slaves without knowing it."

New federal laws have been passed to combat these crimes, but the researchers found that much more needs to be done—especially at the local level. Police officers, rather than federal agents, are most likely to encounter forced labor but often mistake it for illegal immigration and treat victims as part of a criminal enterprise.

The researchers recommend launching a broad-based public awareness campaign; improving monitoring of industries vulnerable to forced labor; increasing training and coordination among law enforcement officials in the United States; and strengthening protections for survivors of forced labor.

The Methodology of the Study

The study was conducted by researchers from Free the Slaves and from the Human Rights Center, which collaborates closely with the International Human Rights Law Clinic at the UC Berkeley School of Law (Boalt Hall). Florida State University's Center for the Advancement of Human Rights also assisted with the research.

The report covers the period of 1998 to 2003 and is based on quantitative and qualitative data, including a survey of 49 service providers experienced in forced labor cases; an analysis of 131 cases of forced labor reported in U.S. newspapers; eight case studies of forced labor in various regions of the United States; and interviews with government officials, service providers and labor advocates. . . .

2

Slavery Is a Serious International Problem

E. Benjamin Skinner

E. Benjamin Skinner is the author of A Crime So Monstrous: Face-to-Face With Modern-Day Slavery.

It may shock many people, but the practice of slavery continues in the contemporary world. It has been estimated that there are more slaves today than at any time in human history. The word "slavery" is frequently used loosely, especially in the United States, but contemporary slavery is a degrading practice. Many who become slaves are born in poverty. Some slaves are stolen from families and forced to work long hours. Slavery even exists in more prosperous countries such as the United States, though the emphasis has often been placed on sex trafficking as opposed to the more common debt bondage. While slavery is widespread today, aggressive actions by governments can recognize and begin putting an end to this most inhuman institution.

One hot June day in 2006, I saw what slavery really meant. In a rundown mansion in a slum of Bucharest, Romania, a pimp offered to sell me a young woman he described as "a blond." She had bleached hair, hastily applied makeup, and she apparently suffered from Down syndrome. On her right arm were at least 10 angry, fresh slashes where, I can only assume, she had attempted suicide. The pimp claimed that he made 200 euros per night renting her out to local clients. He offered to sell her outright to me in exchange for a used car.

E. Benjamin Skinner, "Slavery's Staying Power," *Los Angeles Times*, March 23, 2008. Reproduced by permission.

It wasn't the first time I had encountered a slave in bondage. It wasn't even the first time I had been offered a slave for sale. Over five years on five continents, I had infiltrated trafficking networks and witnessed other negotiations to buy and sell human beings. Worldwide, I'd met more than 100 current and former slaves.

Slavery Today

Many people are surprised to learn that there are still slaves. Many imagined that slavery died along with the 360,000 Union soldiers whose blood fertilized the Emancipation Proclamation and the 13th Amendment. Many thought that slavery was brought to an end around the world when most countries outlawed it in the 19th century.

In the United States today, we tend to use the word "slave" loosely.

But, in fact, there are more slaves today than at any point in history. Although a precise census is impossible, as most masters keep their slaves hidden, baseline estimates from United Nations and other international researchers range from 12 million to 27 million slaves worldwide. The U.S. State Department estimates that from 600,000 to 800,000 people— primarily women and children—are trafficked across national borders each year, and that doesn't count the millions of slaves who are held in bondage within their own countries.

Let me be clear: By "slaves" I mean, very simply, those who are forced to work, under threat of violence, for no pay beyond subsistence. That is the nice, neat, horrible definition I have used since I began studying the subject in 2001. It was brought home to me more vividly than ever by the tears of that young woman in Bucharest.

Defining Slavery

In the United States today, we tend to use the word "slave" loosely. Merriam-Webster offers as its first definition of the word, "drudgery; toil." Well-intentioned activists will say that a worker at a shoe factory in Indonesia is "paid a slave wage" of $1.25 per hour, despite the fact the worker can walk away from the job at any time. An investment banker in New York will claim to be "worked like a slave" because, despite his six-figure salary, he is required to work up to 18 hours a day on occasion. During his last few years with Warner Bros. Records, Prince wore the word "slave" scrawled across his face to protest a binding contract he couldn't get out of—even though it paid him $10-million advances for each album.

But that's not what slavery is, as Rambho Kumar can attest. Kumar was born into wilting poverty in a village in Bihar, the poorest state in India, the country with more slaves than any other, according to U.N. estimates. In 2001, desperate to keep him and his five brothers from starving, his mother accepted 700 rupees ($15) as an advance from a local trafficker, who promised more money once 9-year-old Rambho started working many miles away in India's carpet belt.

After he received Rambho from the trafficker, the loom owner treated his new acquisition like any other low-value industrial tool. He never allowed Rambho and the other slaves to leave the loom, forcing them to work for 19 hours a day, starting at 4 in the morning. The work itself tore into Rambho's small hands, and when he whimpered in pain, the owner's brother stuck his finger in boiling oil to cauterize the wound—and then told him to get back to work. When other boys attempted escape or made a mistake in the intricate designs of the rugs, which were destined for Western markets, the owner beat them savagely.

On July 12, 2005, local police, in coordination with activists supported by Free the Slaves, an organization based in Washington[, D.C.], liberated Rambho and nine other emaciated boys.

I've met and talked with slaves and former slaves like Rambho in a dozen countries, including the United Arab Emirates, Romania, India, Sudan and Haiti. The International Labor Organization of the United Nations estimates that in Asia alone, there are about 10 million slaves.

Slavery in the U.S.

Even in the United States, low-end Justice Department figures estimate that there are about 50,000 people languishing in hidden bondage at any one time. On March 4, [2008,] for instance, two south Florida women were convicted on charges of enslaving and torturing a teenage Haitian girl named Simone Celestine. The two women face 10 years in prison. Celestine was freed by the FBI last year after being held as a domestic slave for six years, during which time she said she was beaten with closed fists, forced to shower outside with a garden hose, rented to other homes and not allowed to attend school.

Celestine's case is eerily similar to that of Williathe Narcisse, a courageous young woman I got to know after she escaped a life of domestic slavery in suburban Miami. Narcisse, who was 12 when she was freed in 1999, had been smuggled into the U.S. from Haiti to work as a domestic servant. During her three years in slavery, she was required to keep the family's home spotless, eat garbage and sleep on the floor. She was repeatedly raped by the family's adult son.

In its first term, the Bush administration spoke out strongly against human trafficking, laying out the most aggressive anti-slavery agenda since Reconstruction. But politics hamstrung its implementation. Pressed by a coalition of academic feminists and evangelical conservatives, American officials focused mainly on eliminating prostitution, despite overwhelming evidence that, worldwide, more than 90% of modern-day slaves are not held in commercial sexual slavery.

Before his reelection, President [George W.] Bush spoke frequently about slavery, including two rousing speeches he gave before the U.N. General Assembly. But in each case, the president only detailed his concern for those in the commercial sex industry, never mentioning debt bondage (in which a person is forced into slavery in order to pay off an initial debt) or labor trafficking. Over the last two years, the State Department's Office to Monitor and Combat Trafficking in Persons has dedicated four times as much of its budget to fighting sex slavery as it did to combating other forms of slavery.

Ending Slavery Today

"It is a vicious myth that women and children who work as prostitutes have voluntarily chosen such a life for themselves," asserted a 2005 State Department fact sheet. Thus the victimization of Ashley Alexandra Dupre, the high-priced call girl frequented by Eliot Spitzer, who . . . was New York's governor, is equated to the slavery of the young woman in the Bucharest brothel.

Even though there are more slaves in the world today than ever, as a percentage of world population, there are fewer than ever. In a generation, bondage could be eradicated. But for this to happen, the U.S. must lead the way.

Slavery in all its forms is a crime against humanity.

First, however, it must define the terms carefully. A current legislative fight is underway about just what slavery means. Over the objections of a few anti-slavery stalwarts in the Justice Department, the House of Representatives passed a bill in December [2007] that expands the current anti-trafficking legislation to cover most forms of prostitution, coerced or not. If approved in its current form by the Senate and signed by the president, the law will no longer address slavery exclusively and will instead become a federal mandate to fight prostitution on a broad scale.

Prostitution is always degrading, and it is often brutal—but it is not always slavery. Equating the scourge of slavery with run-of-the-mill, non-coerced prostitution is not only misleading, it will weaken the world's efforts to end real forced labor and human trafficking.

Slavery in all its forms is a crime against humanity. Rambho's bondage is no more or less tolerable than that of the young woman offered to me in Bucharest. Both are abominations, and both are our collective burden to abolish.

3

Important Facts About Slavery Today

Carolyn Nye

Carolyn Nye has traveled extensively and has been published in Amateur Photography *and* Matador Travel.

Slavery exists today on a global scale, a fact that shocks many who believe that it disappeared long ago. It is difficult for many to comprehend that there are more slaves today than at any time in human history. The recent surge in the practice of slavery has been fueled by the low cost of slaves in many developing nations. It also surprises people that slavery continues to exist in the United States, and that many practices like bonded labor may, in reality, be no different from slavery. A vast criminal enterprise has supported the expansion of slavery, and while the possibility of defeating such an industry may seem daunting, many believe that slavery can be brought to an end in as little as 25 years. Individuals can help bring an end to modern-day slavery by refusing to buy products created by slave labor and by realizing that their actions can make a difference.

2008 witnesses the 200th anniversary of the abolition of the transatlantic slave trade in America. Amidst the celebrations, what many people fail to realize is that slavery persists today in the modern world on an enormous scale.

In spite of the Universal Declaration of Human Rights—adopted by the UN [United Nations] in 1948—stating that

Carolyn Nye, "10 Shocking Facts About Global Slavery," MatadorNetwork.com, 2008. Reproduced by permission.

"slavery and the slave trade shall be prohibited in all their forms," the figures accompanying the modern slave trade seem inconceivable in a global society that prides itself upon its modern-day values and emphasis on human rights.

1. *There are more people in slavery now than at any other time in human history.*

According to research carried out by the organization *Free the Slaves*, more people are enslaved worldwide than ever before.

In its 400 years, the transatlantic slave trade is estimated to have shipped up to 12 million Africans to various colonies in the West. Free the Slaves estimates that the number of people in slavery today is at least 27 million.

People have become disposable and their living conditions are worse than ever before as a result of their value.

The National Underground Railroad Freedom Center suggests that three out of four slavery victims are [female] and that half of all modern-day slaves are children. "Countless other" people are in other forms of servitude which are not legally classified as slavery, according to the Anti-Slavery Society, described ambiguously by some as "unfree labour".

2. *The value of slaves has decreased.*

A slave in 1850 in the American South cost the equivalent of approximately $40,000. According to figures published by FTS [Free the Slaves], the cost of a slave today averages around $90, depending on the work they are forced to carry out.

A young adult male labourer in Mali might [fetch only] $40, whereas an HIV-free female might attract a price of up to $1,000.

Expert Kevin Bales says that because modern slavery is so cheap, it is worse than that of the Atlantic slave trade.

People have become disposable and their living conditions are worse than ever before as a result of their value.

3. *Slavery still exists in the US.*

Estimates by the US State Department suggest up to 17,500 slaves are brought into the US every year [to work] ... as prostitutes, farm workers or domestic servants.

According to the CIA, more than 1,000,000 people are enslaved in the US today. Thousands of cases go undetected each year and many are difficult to take to court as it can be difficult to prove force or legal coercion.

4. *Slavery is hidden behind many other names, thus disguising it from society.*

These names are chattel slavery (the traditional meaning of slavery), bonded labour, trafficking, forced labour, and forced marriage, amongst others.

5. *The least known method of slavery is the most widely used.*

Bonded labour occurs when labour is demanded in order to repay a debt or loan and the cyclical nature of debt and work can enslave the person for the rest of their life. Some conditions are so controlled that slaves are surrounded [while they work] by armed guards ... many of whom are slaves themselves. This has been found in Brazil. It is estimated that there are 20 million bonded labourers in the world.

6. *Human trafficking has recently been described as "the fastest growing criminal enterprise in the world."*

This shocking claim was made by former Secretary of State Madeleine Albright. The UN estimates trafficked human cargo generates around $7 billion ... a year.

7. *To buy all bonded labourers out of slavery could cost as little as $40 per family.*

The $40 figure was provided by the Center for Global Education, New York. Kevin Bales compares the total cost of ending all slavery with one's week's cost of the [U.S.] war [in] Iraq.

8. *Free the Slaves believes it is possible to end all slavery within 25 years.*

Ending slavery won't be easy, but humanity is up to the challenge.

9. *Many slave-produced goods might reach your home without you realizing their origin.*

Industries where slave labour is often highly suspected include cocoa, cotton, steel, oriental rugs, diamonds, and silk. Currently the only way to ensure the products you buy are slave-free is to buy Fair Trade certified goods.

10. *Your actions affect global slavery.*

The bicentennial of the abolition of the slave trade would be better commemorated by every individual taking meaningful action to help end the exploitation of human labour once and for all.

By buying fair trade, learning more about modern slavery, spreading the word, and joining a movement such as Free the Slaves, Anti-Slavery International, or the American Anti-Slavery Group, you as an individual can help abolish slavery completely.

With the number of slaves rising due to increasing economic returns, a universal lack of awareness and anti-slavery laws not being enforced, the National Underground Railroad Freedom Center believes "efforts to combat slavery will have only limited effectiveness" unless something is done on a larger scale.

The bicentennial of the abolition of the slave trade would be better commemorated by every individual taking meaningful action to help end the exploitation of human labour once and for all.

4

Slavery Is Different Today Versus Yesterday

Cassandra Clifford

Cassandra Clifford is the founder and executive director of Bridge to Freedom foundation, which works to enhance and improve the services and opportunities available to survivors of modern slavery.

When people learn that slavery exists in the present world, many wonder how it differs from slavery in the past. Perhaps the biggest difference is that whereas slaves were once expensive acquisitions, today slaves can be bought for very little. This means that slaves who are no longer useful to their owners are disposable. What causes slavery? Poverty, while not the exclusive factor, is often an important one. Many who live in poor circumstances in developing nations offer to pay someone to move them to a more prosperous country. When they arrive in a new country, however, they are told that they are still in debt, or their movement is restricted when traffickers hold the immigrant's passport. Slave labor is now an international problem and is frequently involved in making products that are commonly consumed, such as cocoa. The best way to end the practice of slavery is with education and the development of social and economic alternatives.

W hat is slavery? A horrid word from our past, something we have struggled to forget for almost two hundred years? [It is both] and [neither] of those things, it is a plague

Cassandra Clifford, "Human Slavery Today Versus Yesterday," *Foreign Policy Association* (Blog), April 22, 2007. Reproduced by permission of the author.

currently among us! Would you believe me if I told you we have more slaves today than [in] ... our legal slave trading past?

On January 1, 1863, Lincoln's Emancipation Proclamation was made and ... [freed] approximately four million slaves according to the Census of 1860. Slavery was officially abolished in the United States with the Thirteenth Amendment to the Constitution, passed by Congress on January 31, 1865. The end of slavery in Great Britain officially was passed by Parliament on March 25, 1807.

There are various forms of human slavery today ... [including] debt bondage, sex trafficking, and forced labor.

One does not find the deeds of our ancestors to be noble and just, nor does one find the idea of modern slavery [to be] moral, but the truth of the matter is the problem did not end when it was made an illegal act. As a matter of fact slavery is more rampant today than it was in [the] seventeenth century, as there [are] an estimated 27 million modern slaves today.

Human Slavery Today

Slavery is defined as "The state of one bound in servitude as the property of a slaveholder or household." Kevin Bales states in his book, *Understanding Global Slavery*, that slavery is "the state of control exercised over the slave based on violence or its threat, a lack of any payment beyond subsistence, and the theft of the labor or other qualities of the slave for economic gain" ... Therefore in a general respect slavery is still what it was at the time we began taking slaves out of Africa. However[,] today the crime of slavery has a more seedy and sinister side, as it is the dark underbelly of what is often a complex criminal network, which incorporates the arms and drug trades, that spans the globe.

There are various forms of human slavery today, ... [including] debt bondage, sex trafficking, and forced labor. Children are ... used as soldiers, which is also a form of slavery, as they are forcibly recruited, misguided, abused, and are not of an age to legally make a clear and concise choice.

What is the difference between today's slavery and that [encompassing] the slaves of our past? The largest difference in modern slavery is the lack of value that is placed on a person who is a slave. ... [P]eople have become a disposable commodity, cheap and easy labor one can just toss in the garbage when ... [there is] no longer ... a use for them. They are more often taken into the slave trade for one purpose only, sexual slavery, versus agricultural and domestic labor. This is not to say that we do not have a serious problem with slavery today in those [areas]. But as slaves are cheaper and less valued as ... resources of production, they are often even more dehumanized than in ... our past.

Often the victims return to their homes and are turned away by their families, and are now seen as outcasts by the community.

The use or treatment of slaves differ[s] in some regions or countries ... [and] gender and religion can also play a role in the use and treatment of slaves. However, what remains the same is that ... human being[s are] enslaved by another, stripped of their rights, disrespected, abused and looked upon as subhuman by their owners. The main thing that remains the same is that this practice of selling and abusing another human being is just as appalling today as it was the day the first slave[s were] loaded onto a ship and taken from their home in Africa.

The Cause of Slavery Today

People are often driven into slavery by severe poverty. [S]ometimes this is based on a general belief that ... child[ren] sold will bring money back into the family, or that they will have an honest [opportunity] to escape the poverty of the family and community. Other times people are driven into slavery by economic or social necessity, and they themselves may even be the one who [formed] the idea of working outside the community. Many times ... victim[s] of slavery will even pay a large sum for their travel, and what they believe [are] their visa and placement fees. Unbeknownst to them they are paying money to enslave themselves. These so-called fees are just another way the traffickers and slave owners exploit the victims. If a victim or their family has not put up a sum of money, the traffickers and slave owners use the travel expenses as the beginning of their reign over their victims. Ledgers are kept to show the slave has a debt to work off ... often includ-[ing] the travel and visa expenses the owner has incurred to get the slave and the actual cost they paid for the slave. These ledgers continually mount up the expenses, as housing and food is added to the list, and these so-called ledgers are almost always falsified in the favor of the slave owner. ... [Victims realize] quickly that there is little they can do to pay off the debt they owe, for they supposedly incur more fees than they will ever make. If a victim of slavery does manage to find a way to pay off her debt, the slave owner will more than likely find a way to add additional costs, threaten the victim or their families, or simply re-enslave them.

Victims of slavery and trafficking are often re-enslaved, and I know you are asking yourself, "How is this possible?" The sad reality is that many victims know that their ... owners, or one of their traffickers ... make threats on their families. These threats are very personal and real to the victim[s], as the traffickers often know where the families live, and ... thus they can make them [the victims] succumb again. You must remember these are people who have ... been both physically and mentally abused on a daily basis. Often the victims return to their homes and are turned away by their families, and are now seen as outcasts by the community. Many victims have been drugged heavily while in captivity and are now facing serious addictions and withdrawals, which may lead them back into the world of human slavery. When and if they do return home they again face poverty and hardship, and some are then willing to return to their captors, as they feel they are already so victimized and dead inside that if they can endure this hardship, maybe this time they can go into the sex trade with little to no debts and bring money in for their families.

It is easy to see how this is possible when one looks at various cases of Stockholm Syndrome, where victims of abuse, rape, hostage[taking], etc., become sympathetic, or feel a close bond with their attackers or captors. Many victims of human slavery have been victimized, or enslaved, since an early age, some even since infancy. Therefore it is easy to see how [they] can be accustomed to the only life they have known, even if it is that of a slave. The world is a scary place all on its own, so if a child of 10 runs away from years of slavery, one can clearly see how their past traumas will affect them and could easily lead them to be enslaved by another or return to their original owner.

International Slave Labor

There is not a country out there that is free from slavery. [I]t affects our entire global economy. As individual consumers we are all affected by the slavery of our fellow man, as it is helping to shape our global economy. It is difficult to remember, but when you get something at an unbelievable cost, there is someone out there who is paying that cost for you. According to Jolene Smith, Executive Director of Free the Slaves, our growing economy is what has promoted a large revival of slavery, for as the market increases many people flock to cities around the world in search of better opportunities . . . thus creating millions of vulnerable people.

Products which are often made by the hands of child slave labor include cotton, tea, silk, cocoa, sugar, steel, carpets, diamonds, etc. Products like cocoa/chocolate have been known to be produced with the efforts of child slaves, many [of whom] have been trafficked in Western Africa. [Such products] can only be guaranteed slave-free if they are fair trade. In the report, *Combating Child Labor in Cocoa Growing* conducted by the ILO [International Labour Organization], they estimate 200,000 children work on cocoa farms in the Ivory Coast. The Ivory Coast is the worst offender in the cocoa and slave trade today. Coffee has had a heavy past using slave labor, [but] it has seen a turnaround with the ever-growing and consci[enti]ous public buying fair trade coffee products. In the article "Is There Slavery in Your Chocolate?" Gary Goldstein of the National Coffee Association said:

"This industry isn't responsible for what happens in a foreign country."

Companies like M&M Mars and [Hershey's], both [of] who[m] claim there is little they can do to change the labor practices of the farms they purchase from . . . use slave-grown cocoa. Chocolate is now receiving a lot of . . . public [attention,] and now campaigns are increasing to see that consumers buy slave-free chocolate. And while buying fair trade helps immensely, it alone is not a solution to the problem, and let's face it, most consumers will continue to buy the mass-produced name brands. The main reason we really buy slave products, is that as consumers we are unaware. For is price really an option when it comes to the freedom of another human?

The only true way to end slavery is education and alternative solutions, both [social] and [economic].

Which countries are big in the use of slave labor? Well, the list, I am afraid, is too long to go into in depth in this [essay], but the largest contributing country for slave labor is India. African nations have a large number of slaves. [S]laves can be found in Saudi Arabia, Pakistan, China, Nepal, and . . . many more [countries], including the United States.

Companies with a slave labor history of producing or purchasing raw materials or end products include M&M Mars, [Hershey's], Folgers, Wal-Mart, Nike, Tommy Hilfiger USA, Gap (including Old Navy and Banana Republic), Calvin Klein and Liz Claiborne. [These] are just some of the companies that have in some [way] benefited from the use of slave labor.

Education and Alternative Solutions

Now you are probably asking yourself: "How do you stay slave free as a consumer?" "Who do you avoid and what don't you buy?" "How do you know something is slave free?" "Which countries do you watch products from?" And the truth is, regardless of how much you try to avoid it, you cannot escape slavery. I am sure if I go through my things there is something that is slave made or was in part produced by the slave trade. All-out boycotts don't work, as they only exacerbate the situation most of the time. [T]hey carry too much risk as they can cause current slaves in the boycotted industry to become enslaved again in a new industry. However, as I mentioned, being aware and being . . . consci[enti]ous as a consumer and a citizen is the right start.

The only true way to end slavery is education and alternative solutions, both [social] and [economic]. Knowledge and education are key, we must be aware [of] and make sure everyone is aware of the risks, the true nature of the struggle, and [the] reality that this is a huge issue. We have to stop slavery at its root. [S]lavery continues to thrive in the modern world because [of] its high level of profitability! And, unfortunately, for many traffickers and slave owners the risks are low, and as long as there is low risk and high profitability, combined with economic necessity, then the trafficking and slavery of other human beings will continue!

We can end human slavery and suffering worldwide, and we must. The first step is admitting that the issue is a major one that is facing every corner of the globe. Pay attention: you never know when you may witness a victim of human slavery.

5

Human Trafficking Assumes Many Forms

Office to Monitor and Combat Trafficking in Persons

The Office to Monitor and Combat Trafficking in Persons is a federal government agency that focuses on the eradication of modern-day slavery.

Because modern-day slavery and human trafficking assume many forms in the United States and abroad, they are often difficult to detect. These forms include, but are not limited to, forced labor, bonded labor, involuntary domestic servitude, forced child labor, child soldiers, and sex trafficking. Many persons are forced into slavery once they become indebted to traffickers; others, like some domestic workers and children, are held by threat of violence. Enslavement even involves recruiting and abducting children into the military, and exploiting children for prostitution and sex tourism.

The hidden nature of trafficking in persons prevents a precise count of the number of victims around the world, but available research indicates that, when trafficking within a country's borders is included in the count, more people fall victim to labor forms of trafficking than sex trafficking. Although labor trafficking and sex trafficking are usually analyzed as separate trafficking-in-persons issues, victims of both forms of trafficking often share a common denominator: their trafficking ordeal started with a migration in search of economic alternatives.

Office to Monitor and Combat Trafficking in Persons, "Major Forms of Trafficking in Persons," *Trafficking in Persons Report 2008*, Washington, D.C.: U.S. Department of State, June 4, 2008.

The theme of migration is often heard in reporting on trafficking in persons and indeed the movement of victims is a common trait in many trafficking crimes. Yet servitude can also occur without the movement of a person. In analyzing trafficking in persons issues and designing effective responses, the focus should be on the exploitation and control of a person through force, fraud, or coercion—not on the movement of that person.

Neither the international definition of trafficking in persons, as defined in the 2000 UN [United Nations] Protocol to Prevent, Suppress, and Punish Trafficking in Persons, Especially Women and Children, nor the U.S. definition of severe forms of trafficking in persons, as defined in federal law, requires the movement of the victim. Movement is not necessary, as any person who is recruited, harbored, provided, or obtained through force, fraud, or coercion for the purpose of subjecting that person to involuntary servitude, forced labor, or commercial sex qualifies as a trafficking victim.

Domestic servitude is particularly difficult to detect because it occurs in private homes, which are often unregulated by public authorities.

Major Forms of Trafficking in Persons

Forced Labor. Most instances of forced labor occur as unscrupulous employers take advantage of gaps in law enforcement to exploit vulnerable workers. These workers are made more vulnerable to forced labor practices because of unemployment, poverty, crime, discrimination, corruption, political conflict, and cultural acceptance of the practice. Immigrants are particularly vulnerable, but individuals are also forced into labor in their own countries. Female victims of forced or bonded labor, especially women and girls in domestic servitude, are often sexually exploited as well. Forced labor is a form of human trafficking that can be harder to identify and estimate than sex trafficking. It may not involve the same criminal networks profiting from transnational sex trafficking, but may instead involve individuals who subject anywhere from one to hundreds of workers to involuntary servitude, perhaps through forced or coerced household work or work at a factory.

Bonded Labor. One form of force or coercion is the use of a bond, or debt, to keep a person under subjugation. This is referred to in law and policy as "bonded labor" or "debt bondage." It is criminalized under U.S. law and included as a form of exploitation related to trafficking in the UN TIP [Trafficking in Persons] Protocol. Many workers around the world fall victim to debt bondage when traffickers or recruiters unlawfully exploit an initial debt the worker assumed as part of the terms of employment, or when workers inherit debt in more traditional systems of bonded labor. Traditional bonded labor in South Asia enslaves huge numbers of people from generation to generation.

Debt Bondage and Involuntary Servitude Among Migrant Laborers. The vulnerability of migrant laborers to trafficking schemes is especially disturbing because this population is so sizeable in some regions. Three potential contributors can be discerned: 1) Abuse of contracts; 2) Inadequate local laws governing the recruitment and employment of migrant laborers; and 3) The intentional imposition of exploitative and often illegal costs and debts on these laborers in the source country or state, often with the complicity and/or support of labor agencies and employers in the destination country or state.

Some abuses of contracts and hazardous conditions of employment do not in themselves constitute involuntary servitude, though use or threat of physical force or restraint to compel a worker to enter into or continue labor or service may convert a situation into one of forced labor. Costs imposed on laborers for the "privilege" of working abroad can place laborers in a situation highly vulnerable to debt bondage. However, these costs alone do not constitute debt bondage or involuntary servitude. When combined with exploitation by unscrupulous labor agents or employers in the destination country, these costs or debts, when excessive, can become a form of debt bondage.

Involuntary Domestic Servitude. Domestic workers may be trapped in servitude through the use of force or coercion, such as physical (including sexual) or emotional abuse. Children are particularly vulnerable. Domestic servitude is particularly difficult to detect because it occurs in private homes, which are often unregulated by public authorities. For example, there is great demand in some wealthier countries of Asia and the Middle East for domestic servants who sometimes fall victim to conditions of involuntary servitude.

Forced Child Labor. Most international organizations and national laws recognize that children may legally engage in light work. In contrast, the worst forms of child labor are being targeted for eradication by nations across the globe. The sale and trafficking of children and their entrapment in bonded and forced labor are clearly among the worst forms of child labor. Any child who is subject to involuntary servitude, debt bondage, peonage, or slavery through the use of force, fraud, or coercion is a victim of trafficking in persons regardless of the location of that exploitation.

Using Children as Combatants

Child Soldiers. Child soldiering is a unique and severe manifestation of trafficking in persons that involves the unlawful recruitment of children through force, fraud, or coercion to be exploited for their labor or to be abused as sex slaves in conflict areas. Such unlawful practices may be perpetrated by government forces, paramilitary organizations, or rebel groups. UNICEF [the United Nations Children's Fund] estimates that more than 300,000 children under 18 are currently being exploited in more than 30 armed conflicts worldwide. While the majority of child soldiers are between the ages of 15 and 18, some are as young as 7 or 8 years of age.

Many children are abducted to be used as combatants. Others are made unlawfully to serve as porters, cooks, guards, servants, messengers, or spies. Many young girls are forced to marry or have sex with male combatants and are at high risk of unwanted pregnancies. Male and female child soldiers are often sexually abused and are at high risk of contracting sexually transmitted diseases.

Each year, more than two million children are exploited in the global commercial sex trade.

Some children have been forced to commit atrocities against their families and communities. Child soldiers are often killed or wounded, with survivors often suffering multiple traumas and psychological scarring. Their personal development is often irreparably damaged. Returning child soldiers are often rejected by their home communities.

Child soldiers are a global phenomenon. The problem is most critical in Africa and Asia, but armed groups in the Americas and the Middle East also unlawfully use children in conflict areas. All nations must work together with international organizations and NGOs [nongovernmental organizations] to take urgent action to disarm, demobilize, and reintegrate child soldiers.

Commercial Sex Industry Creates Demand

Sex Trafficking and Prostitution. Sex trafficking comprises a significant portion of overall trafficking and the majority of transnational modern-day slavery. Sex trafficking would not exist without the demand for commercial sex flourishing around the world. The U.S. Government adopted a strong position against prostitution in a December 2002 policy decision, which notes that prostitution is inherently harmful and dehumanizing, and fuels trafficking in persons. Turning people into dehumanized commodities creates an enabling environment for human trafficking.

The United States Government opposes prostitution and any related activities, including pimping, pandering, or maintaining brothels as contributing to the phenomenon of trafficking in persons, and maintains that these activities should not be regulated as a legitimate form of work for any human being. Those who patronize the commercial sex industry form a demand which traffickers seek to satisfy.

Children Exploited for Commercial Sex. Each year, more than two million children are exploited in the global commercial sex trade. Many of these children are trapped in prostitution. The commercial sexual exploitation of children is trafficking, regardless of circumstances. International covenants and protocols obligate criminalization of the commercial sexual exploitation of children. The use of children in the commercial sex trade is prohibited under both U.S. law and the U.N. TIP Protocol. There can be no exceptions, no cultural or socioeconomic rationalizations that prevent the rescue of children from sexual servitude. Terms such as "child sex worker" are unacceptable because they falsely sanitize the brutality of this exploitation.

Child Sex Tourism. Child-sex tourism (CST) involves people who travel from their own country—often a country where child sexual exploitation is illegal or culturally abhorrent—to another country where they engage in commercial sex acts with children. CST is a shameful assault on the dignity of children and a form of violent child abuse. The commercial sexual exploitation of children has devastating consequences for minors, which may include long-lasting physical and psychological trauma, disease (including HIV/AIDS), drug addiction, unwanted pregnancy, malnutrition, social ostracism, and possibly death.

Tourists engaging in CST often travel to developing countries looking for anonymity and the availability of children in prostitution. The crime is typically fueled by weak law enforcement, corruption, the Internet, ease of travel, and poverty. Sex offenders come from all socio-economic backgrounds and may in some cases hold positions of trust. Cases of child sex tourism involving U.S. citizens have included a pediatrician, a retired Army sergeant, a dentist, and a university professor. Child pornography is frequently involved in these cases, and drugs may also be used to solicit or control the minors.

6

Sex Slavery Is Practiced in the United States

Catherine Edwards

Catherine Edwards is a writer for Insight on the News.

Human trafficking for the sex trade is a worldwide industry that also affects the United States. An estimated 700,000 women are enslaved on a global scale, and an estimated 50,000 of them will come to the United States. Many of these women are lured into trafficking under the false promises of employment; once they arrive in a new country, they are ensnared by traffickers and forced into prostitution. Many barriers, including language, make it difficult for them to leave.

The [George W.] Bush administration, working with Congress and the State and Justice departments, is organizing a war against violent international-and slavery rings.

Movement of women and children from one country to another, or within national borders, for sexual exploitation or forced labor is called trafficking. For the first seven months of the [George W.] Bush administration its abolition has had a high priority. According to Interpol, profits from this trade top $19 billion annually. Congressional sources estimate that 50,000 persons are trafficked into the United States annually and 2 million worldwide. The United Nations puts the number worldwide at 4 million.

Investigative journalist Christine Dolan recently spent several months in Europe looking into this human trafficking for

Catherine Edwards, "Sex-Slave Trade Is Thriving," *Insight on the News*, vol. 17, no. 30, August 13, 2001, pp. 16–17. Copyright © 2001 News World Communications, Inc. All rights reserved. Reproduced with permission of *Insight*.

the International Center for Missing and Exploited Children. She found that not only are women and children being trafficked for sexual purposes, but also infants and toddlers. In her report, "A Shattered Innocence: The Millennium Holocaust," she calls for a declaration of war on the mobsters, pimps and other criminals who are responsible.

Many of these victims . . . are lured by promises of gainful employment in the United States . . . only to find themselves kidnapped, raped and sold into prostitution . . .

Dolan applauds the U.S. government for what is being done to resist this exploitation but insists the problem is at the local level where law enforcement is badly in need of training. "They know the local mob, they know their neighborhood, but they don't have the specialized training to outwit these international criminals," Dolan says.

The U.S. State Department released its first Annual Trafficking in Persons Report in mid-July, as mandated by Congress last year in the Victims of Violence and Trafficking Protection Act of 2000. This law requires the State Department to expand the annual human-rights reports to cover severe forms of trafficking in persons and to create an interagency task force to coordinate efforts nationally and internationally to stop it.

Curiously, in this first report the State Department claims that only 700,000 people a year are being trafficked as sex slaves or as sweatshop workers, much lower than any other estimate. It does, however, confirm Insight's reports that many of these victims, whatever their number, are lured by promises of gainful employment in the, such as waitress jobs or jobs as dancers or models, only to find themselves kidnapped, raped and sold into prostitution once they arrive (see "Sex Slave Trade Enters the U.S.," Nov. 27, 2000).

Last year's legislation was the first passed in recent years to combat human trafficking. Previously the Department of Justice (DOJ) prosecuted traffickers under the old antislavery and peonage laws. The annual report it requires, say Capitol Hill sources, is supposed to monitor the problem while alerting the American people. "This report is one volley in that global fight for freedom of countless people," says Sen. Sam Brownback, R-Kan., one of the bill's sponsors.

"International sex trafficking is the new slavery," Brownback says. "It includes the classic and awful elements associated with historic slavery, such as abduction from family and home, use of false promises, transport to a strange country, loss of freedom and personal dignity, extreme abuse and deprivation."

Attorney General John Ashcroft told reporters in February that fighting sex trafficking would be a priority of the DOJ during his tenure. Only 16 cases have been prosecuted in the United States since 1999, and in mid-July the attorney general issued regulations to provide assistance and protection to victims of human trafficking while their cases are investigated and prosecuted. The new rules not only enable federal law-enforcement personnel and immigration officials to protect victims, but they require and outline related training for DOJ and State Department personnel and mandate interdepartmental cooperation.

"The cooperative efforts of federal agencies and law-enforcement officials will help provide victims the tools and services needed to punish traffickers to the fullest extent of the law," Ashcroft told reporters.

Two cases so far have been prosecuted under the new law and regulations. In March a man named Kill Soo Lee was arrested in American Samoa on a two-count federal complaint charging violations of slavery statutes. Lee held mostly female workers from Vietnam in involuntary servitude at his garment factory. That same month a landlord in Berkeley, Calif., pleaded guilty to trafficking women into the United States and placing them in sexual servitude. In February, Michael Allen Lee was charged with having forced homeless African-American men to work in his Florida fields. That same month Jose Tekum of Florida was sentenced to nine years in prison for felony counts that included kidnapping, slavery and immigration violations and forcing a Guatemalan woman to engage in sex acts and manual labor against her will.

Because the new law requires that official assistance be given to victims on U.S. soil and directs the Justice Department among other agencies to administer this, the DOJ has set up a telephone help-line. Callers may report cases of trafficking or slavery to the National Worker Exploitation Task Force by calling (888) 428-7581 weekdays, 9 A.M. to 5 P.M. EST.

Secretary of State Colin Powell will chair a Cabinet-level interagency task force on trafficking. A State Department spokesman tells Insight that there will be an office to act as the working group for the task force. The task force has not met yet, but State already is pursuing countertrafficking measures, the spokesman says.

"The biggest problem we face is to convince people that this is actually taking place . . ."

As many as 5,000 aliens trafficked into the United States by organized-crime syndicates will be permitted to remain on a new nonimmigrant visa, provided they assist in the investigation of their perpetrators, are younger than age 15 or can demonstrate that they would suffer severe harm if returned to their country of origin. The Office of Victims of Crime at DOJ is funding a pilot project headed by the Coalition to Abolish Slavery and Trafficking, a private organization offering assistance to victims of trafficking in Los Angeles.

Meanwhile, President George W. Bush can impose nontrade, nonhumanitarian sanctions against countries that do not comply with minimum standards to eliminate trafficking. The countries that currently have no laws against forced labor and prostitution have four years to enact such laws before being vulnerable to application of sanctions, but the president can waive such sanctions at any time.

The State Department's annual report on this problem not only includes trafficking data gathered by the State Department from the 185 diplomatic posts worldwide, but updates Congress on progress being made by each country to combat trafficking. It also lists antitrafficking groups that have received federal funds to carry out their work.

The State Department compiled three lists of countries. Tier 1 countries are those that fully comply with minimum standards, as described in the U.S. law, that successfully prosecute trafficking and that provide assistance to victims. These include Austria, Canada, Taiwan and the United Kingdom. Tier 2 countries are those that do not fully comply with the minimum standards but are taking steps to bring themselves into compliance. State claims these include Angola, Bangladesh, China, India, Morocco, Thailand and Vietnam. Tier 3 countries do not comply with the minimum standards and are making no effort to do so. They include Albania, Bosnia, Burma, Indonesia, Pakistan, Qatar, Saudi Arabia and the United Arab Emirates. A full listing is available from the State Department at www.state.gov.

Brownback tells Insight that he will use the information about the trafficking practices of each country to press the issue with their governments and recommend its use to the attorney general as guidance in training U.S law enforcement about the global magnitude of the problem. "The biggest problem we face is to convince people that this is actually taking place," Brownback says. "So I applaud the attorney general for making it a top priority when he has hundreds of things to work on."

As a result of her investigation, Dolan recently launched a group called the International Humanitarian Campaign Against the Exploitation of Children, which may be contacted on the Internet at www.helpsavekids.org. It will raise money for training local law enforcement about the problem, get rape counselors for safe houses to counsel trafficked children and raise awareness globally. "This is a transcontinental and trans-criminal problem," says Dolan. "These are criminals with no compassion, no respect for human life."

How bad are these people? Dolan interviewed a trafficker in Albania named Alberto who said he trafficked for the quick money. He had been doing it for two years and moved his "stock" between Antwerp, Brussels and Belgium. Alberto said young girls bring very high prices. When asked how young, all he would say was, "Very young, very young."

"People are not like tobacco and drugs, which once sold are used and literally go up in smoke," says Dolan. "As long as human beings are alive they can be used and abused at every step of the trafficking game, being sold and resold."

7

Human Trafficking in the United States is Difficult to Document

Cathy Young

Cathy Young is a contributing editor for Reason *magazine.*

At the beginning of 2004, the New York Times Magazine *published an article on sexual slavery in the United States, estimating that 30,000 to 50,000 women had been forced into prostitution. But while sexual slavery certainly exists in the United States, and while any form of slavery is a horrible thing, questions remain about the validity of the numbers. Many of the claims in the article were difficult to substantiate, and it was impossible to separate those who chose to work in prostitution from those who were forced to work in prostitution. While it is worthy to try to bring attention to a social problem such as sexual slavery, sensational claims can serve as a detriment to addressing the problem.*

The latest controversy to erupt in journalism centers on a story about what everyone agrees is a real and serious problem: sexual slavery in which women and sometimes children are forced into prostitution. The question is whether a recent *New York Times Magazine* cover story exaggerated the scope of this ugly phenomenon, and whether author Peter Landesman was too uncritical in reporting the claims of agenda-driven activists. Landesman's lengthy article, "The

Cathy Young, "Sex Suckers: Activists Hoodwink Gray Lady," *Reason Online*, February 10, 2004. Reproduced by permission of the author.

Girls Next Door," has been extensively analyzed by Jack Shafer at *Slate*. Shafer notes that while Landesman refers to only two criminal cases involving forced prostitution, he depicts sexual slavery as an epidemic raging unseen in seemingly respectable neighborhoods.

No one disputes that sexual slavery exists, or that it is a terrible thing.

The article acknowledges that the government has no information on how many women are trafficked annually into the United States for purposes of prostitution, yet goes on to cite alarming figures: 10,000 sex slaves imported every year, and a total of 30,000 to 50,000 slaves living in the country. These figures are based on estimates by anti-slavery and anti-trafficking activists such as Kevin Bales of the nonprofit organization Free the Slaves and Laura Lederer, a feminist attorney who has also crusaded against pornography.

Lurid and Sensational Claims

Shafer and other critics point out that Landesman never witnessed any forced prostitution firsthand. He offers no corroboration for many lurid and sensational claims—for instance, that some sexual slavery rings allow clients to kill a child for a fee, or that women and children are routinely murdered by traffickers. One woman he profiles as a former sex slave, Andrea, offers a tale somewhat reminiscent of the now-debunked "recovered memories" about ritual abuse in satanic cults.

Andrea, who says she spent 12 years in captivity after being sold or abandoned by her mother at about age four, claims that her captors/pimps would sometimes turn her over to clients at Disneyland, dressing her in a specific color so they could identify her.

A *New York Times* editor has subsequently stated that Andrea's story was corroborated to the magazine's fact-checkers by Andrea's therapist; but is that a reliable journalistic source? (Many therapists believe it is their obligation to take a client's narratives at face value.) An additional red flag is raised by Landesman's statement on a radio show that Andrea suffers from multiple personality disorder—a common marker of false memories of sexual abuse.

The reality of sexual trafficking is complex and disturbing.

A Complex and Disturbing Reality

Again, no one disputes that sexual slavery exists, or that it is a terrible thing. There are known cases in which young women from Mexico, Russia, Eastern Europe, and other countries have been lured to the United States with promises of jobs or marriage, and were forced into prostitution and robbed of all their earnings. Late last month [January 2004], the Justice Department announced the indictment of three men who allegedly operated such a ring.

But the reality of sexual trafficking is complex and disturbing. Some women are coerced into prostitution; others choose it as what they hope will be the ticket to a better life. These choices may be the product of hard and even desperate circumstances, but that's not the same thing as forced prostitution. A recent article in *Time* magazine highlights the difficulty of combating this problem. In October, nationwide raids in the Czech Republic to free women from sexual slavery—an operation in which over 4,000 people were interviewed— netted only 15 arrests and three women who asked to return to their countries of origin. Thousands of migrant prostitutes are deported each year from European Union countries only to return again and again.

The activists against sexual slavery on whom Landesman relied so heavily in compiling information for his article are engaged in an admirable cause. But, like many advocates, they can be blinded by their agenda. Lederer, for instance, tells Landesman that "We're not finding victims [of sexual slavery] in the United States because we're not looking for them"—a statement that has some truth in it, but may also be a convenient way to explain the lack of evidence. The numbers touted by these activists are especially suspect since many of them deliberately blur the lines between voluntary and forced prostitution, regarding all of it as servitude and exploitation of women.

There is no doubt that Landesman's article was a well-intentioned effort. But its unraveling illustrates some common pitfalls of which all journalists should beware. One is the temptation to sensationalize the plight of sympathetic victims. Another is checking skepticism at the front door when confronted with the claims of activists for noble causes, be it homelessness, domestic violence, or sexual slavery.

8

Enormity of Slavery Problem Overwhelms Aid Workers

Scott Carrier

Scott Carrier is an independent radio producer and writer whose work has appeared in Rolling Stone.

Human trafficking has flourished around the world in poor countries such as Cambodia and Vietnam. The United Nations has estimated the number of victims to be between 600,000 and 800,000. But while everyone realizes that trafficking is a major problem on the international scene, no one believes that there is a workable solution. In countries such as Cambodia, many laws are not enforced because of political corruption. As a result, it is not uncommon to find markets or brothels of young girls set up in public spaces. Although many individuals and government officials work for change, they frequently become overwhelmed by the enormity of the task. Instead of solving the problem of human trafficking, they are simply left to help its victims in small ways.

I think of this rice field at sunset, out in the countryside. I'm with Lisa and the sun is going down and the sky is dark with storm clouds on the horizon, but the long grass is glowing, luminescent, and there's a water buffalo caked with mud standing motionless by the side of the road staring me straight in the eye. Two men are riding by on heavy Chinese bicycles, each wearing sandals and shorts and a headlamp powered by

Scott Carrier, "In a Brothel Atop Street 63: The Intimate Face of Slavery in Cambodia— Where Buying and Selling Children Is a Family Business," *Mother Jones*, March 1, 2006. Reproduced by permission.

a six-pound battery slung over his shoulder, each holding a wooden spear against the handlebars. Frog hunters. And from far away—a mile across fields and trees—an electric guitar and the bass notes to "Oye Como Va" played karaoke style.

There's a village of wooden huts built up on stilts—cows and chickens underneath, pigs in a pen around back, fruit trees, vegetable gardens, marijuana plants. Lots of kids running around, babies on their sisters' backs. Dogs barking. Mosquitoes. The men come and we eat dinner sitting cross-legged in a circle—one of the chickens and some of the vegetables in a noodle soup made with ganja buds, a specialty for Lisa, who says her stomach has been acting up. The men are joking and laughing, pouring shot glasses of homemade alcohol and making toasts where every glass touches. The two oldest men are in their mid-50s and one is wearing a hat with a bald eagle and an American flag. I ask him if the Americans bombed this area in the early '70s, and he says not this village but in the mountains nearby there were a lot of bombs. "And you still like America?" I ask. He says, "Yes, of course. I fought with the Americans as a Lon Nol soldier." He tells me the man whose house we are eating in also fought as a Lon Nol soldier, but he died four months ago from AIDS. He and the other men believe his ghost is still here, that he hasn't left yet. We toast the ghost, and it gets quiet, except for the crickets.

After dinner, we walk through a couple of gardens to a small hut made from bamboo poles and thatched palm fronds. There's no light inside, completely dark, but there's a voice, like a rock being rolled through dry grass, and the room smells as if an animal has died. Someone brings a light, a 29-watt fluorescent tube on the end of a long extension cord. The woman is at least 80 years old, white hair, skin and bones, lying on a wooden bed without a mattress, blanket, or pillow. Her eyes are moist and cloudy. She sits up and holds her arms around her shins. The toes on her right foot have swollen to twice the size of the toes on her left foot, and there's a three-inch square of skin on the top of her foot that has turned to mushy liquid, pureed salmon. Above the infection, the skin is a black flame, turning green and yellow. Gangrene. She says it hurts.

Worldwide, people are cheaper now than ever before, and there seems to be an endless supply as well as an endless demand.

There's no money for a doctor or a hospital. Traditional ointments and teas did nothing to stop the infection.

Lisa sits down next to the old lady, takes her leg gently in her hands, and speaks to her in Khmer. Lisa is an American who produces public service commercials and documentaries for Cambodian television. She knows nothing of medicine, doesn't know the woman has gangrene, but she does know she's dying—slowly and painfully—she can feel it, and she tries to comfort her. I'm frightened by the whole thing and turn around and there are 12 children pressed together just inside the door, all motionless and absolutely quiet, eyes fixed on Lisa's hands, all wondering if this American woman who is tall and beautiful can cure their great-grandmother. Maybe she has magical power. I can't quite take it and step through the kids to get some fresh air and listen to the dogs bark. Next door there's another, larger hut, and inside a man is sitting on a stool two feet from a 12-inch television screen. He's glued to it, as if manning a periscope. The screen shows new cars and houses with carpets and refrigerators, beautiful people with stylish clothes, women with lipstick. It shows this world, another planet, where there's lots of cool stuff and money, a place where grandmothers do not die slowly, painfully, in the dark, from gangrene.

Human Trafficking Today

This is how what we now call human trafficking begins. It's an awkward term, borrowed from the black market for drugs and guns, only in this case it means the buying and selling of human beings. We used to call it slavery, but the United Nations and the U.S. State Department thought we needed a new name because it's become such a big business. Worldwide, people are cheaper now than ever before, and there seems to be an endless supply as well as an endless demand.

The causes are said to be exploding populations, increasing power differentials between the rich and the poor, corrupt governments, failed states . . . and television, which functions like a huge suction machine, a black hole, pulling people away from shrinking farms and into swollen cities. It starts as migration, a children's crusade for some of that stuff to bring back home. They leave the village and give themselves up to the great sky of luck; they take a chance. And it ends, too often, with young people being bought and consumed and thrown away like a candy bar and its wrapper. And this is also a cause: the desire, the pull for more cheap bodies, whether they are put to work in garment factories and paid 15 cents an hour for 90 hours a week, or thrown onto Thai fishing boats and fed methamphetamines for a few years then shot and thrown overboard, or sold into prostitution or domestic service in Sweden, the United States, or Saudi Arabia. The supply and the demand, the push and the pull, are inseparable.

Nobody knows the numbers. Slaves, unlike guns or drugs, are hard to see and count. Is this boy on your fishing boat an employee? Is this girl a willing prostitute? Is your maid free to leave the house? No one tells the truth. The United Nations claims that every year 600,000 to 800,000 men, women, and children are trafficked as slaves across international boundaries and millions more are sold as slaves within their own countries, but experts in the field say these numbers are inflated to gather public awareness. None of the experts, however, deny that there is a serious problem. And many, if not most, have gone past the point of believing in a solution. . . .

The Politics of Trafficking

According to the United Nations, human trafficking includes "the recruitment, transportation, transfer, harboring or receipt of persons, by means of threat or use of force or other forms of coercion, of abduction, of fraud, of deception, of the abuse of power or of a position of vulnerability or of the giving or receiving of payments or benefits to achieve the consent of a person having control over another person. . . ." It goes on and on, passing through a difficult section about the selling of people for use as sexual slaves and ending with "the removal of organs."

Off the record, people within the U.S. State Department in Cambodia will tell you they don't know what human trafficking is or how it happens. And yet their job is to get rid of it. They say they have more anti-trafficking money than they know what to do with, that there aren't enough aid workers in the country to give the money to, and consequently much of the money is being given to faith-based initiatives. They call this cronyism, like it's an infectious disease.

The other side of this, however, is that Cambodia is actually way f---d up. Mothers really do sell their kids. Little babies are sold for adoption, girls as young as eight are sold for their virginity, boys are sold to beg on the streets of Bangkok and Saigon, or thrown onto fishing boats, never to come back. It happens, a lot, and nobody does anything to stop it. Not really. Cambodia is the first country in the world to create a special police task force to fight human trafficking, and in the four years of its existence, the number of arrests for sexual trafficking offenses has increased from 40 to over 600 a year. This sounds like a positive statistic until you realize that the justice system in Cambodia is just a pretense for extracting money from the accused, who are expected to buy their way out of jail. A debauchery rap now costs $20,000. The accused hires a lawyer, from jail, and the lawyer pays off the court clerk, the prosecutor, and the judge. The records of the court proceedings—like, for instance, the number of successful convictions for trafficking-related offenses—these documents are said to rest in the possession of one man, National Chief of Police Hok Lundy, and he has not been inclined to release them.

The political system in Cambodia is shaped like a pyramid, where the people on the top can commit unspeakable crimes and the people on the bottom have no rights at all. Money, in the form of bribes and extortions, flows upward through the pyramid, and violence comes back down. This is the cultural mechanism of impunity. It's where the slaves come from. The U.S. State Department has published in its 2004 report on human trafficking that high-ranking members of the Cambodian government are directly involved in, and profit from, the sale of human beings—among the aid workers monitoring the trafficking, this is a well-known fact. The names are known but they are not spoken. There is silence in the face of evil, and under this silence the phrase "human trafficking" becomes a bull---- term, propaganda, a way of labeling something we don't understand in order to throw a lot of money at it while loudly saying we are winning the war against it.

Mothers really do sell their kids.

Open Markets For Girls

I'll tell you about two places I saw. One was an open-air market for girls at a place called the Chicken Farm outside Koh Kong, a town on the southwestern coast. There's a river and a port, ships coming and going from the Gulf of Siam. The road coming into Koh Kong is dirt and impassable at times during the rainy season, but the road going out of Koh Kong, over a bridge and across the border into Thailand, is concrete and busy with truck traffic. The Chicken Farm is out in a field near the river, or that's how I imagined it. I couldn't see a thing, the night was so dark—no moon, no stars, just the dim outlines of six or seven huts and the doorways glowing red, small shrines lit by candles out front, the smell of burning incense. The girls sat in pods of light from fluorescent tubes—six in front of me, eight next door, five across the road. They came from the farmlands of Cambodia and Vietnam, 12 to 16 years old, all for sale. "Cheap, good price," the pimp tells me. "You want boom boom, $15. You want take, you keep, no problem. Good price, you say."

The other place was on Street 63 in Phnom Penh, right in the middle of the city, not far from the U.N. [United Nations] offices and the shopping mall. It's a room up two flights of steep steps, a room that could have once been a classroom or even a small dance studio, and there are 20 girls, fifth-graders, sitting in chairs in a big circle around me. Their faces covered with white makeup, purple lipstick. All from Vietnam. None are virgins. One is straddling my thigh, with her arms around my neck, and I can't look at her and I'm trying not to hear the few words she's saying. The others are laughing and giggling with each other, and when I make eye contact, their smiles turn to fear. They are supposed to flirt with me, but they're not even old enough to know how to flirt and they're scared—scared that I might choose them and scared that I might not and they'll be beaten. At that moment, I would [rather have] been almost anywhere else, but to make it worse, in walks another man, an American by his dress, early '60s, like he'd just come in from playing golf. He sits down next to me but does not make eye contact, and at that point I stop breathing. I'm there to look, but he's there for the real thing and I should hold it together and try to talk to him, find out what he thinks he's doing, but I bolt for the door and the girls all instantly freak out and start screaming in terror. They stand in front of me and I have to pull arms off my waist and tear hands off my shirt, and just as I get to the stairs, the pimp blocks my way and says I can't leave. I grab him by the arms and hold him out over the stairs and ask him if he wants me to let go. This calms him down and I run out of there, demons flying, chasing me out the door.

It's creepy, for sure, but the thing that's really unnerving is that it happens right out in the open. It's no secret to anybody, and yet no one does anything to stop it. You walk away from it, and there's a tearing sound, like the ripping of fabric that goes on and on and will not stop.

Working For Change

Lisa is making a video documentary about human trafficking, an Asia Foundation/USAID [United States Agency for International Development] project for the Cambodian television audience. She wanted to go to these places with me, but she couldn't, not without setting off all the alarms, so to speak. So I tell her about what I saw and she freaks out on me. She's my guide, really the best I could ask for, but she sometimes breaks down in tears. I think this is common among NGO [nongovernmental organization] workers and diplomats in Cambodia. They spend their days trying to help people, trying to rebuild the country, and many spend their nights trying to drink and dance away the despair that comes from knowing their efforts are failing. The men often descend into hard drugs and prostitutes; the women become lonely and emotionally wounded. It's tough—tough to sleep through the hot humid nights, tough to face the street in the morning.

I tell Lisa what I saw and she falls apart. She has a number of powers—charm and grace and also the talent or curse of the empath. She can feel what others feel, and apparently just my descriptions can make her become one of the Vietnamese girls with white faces.

"I think they're reptilian," she says. "They use that part of their brain. You're always on the bottom tier, always a pain in your stomach. You ever been hungry for days at a time? Do you know what that feels like?"

She's been here more than four years. She's made friends with a lot of people—from kids who scavenge the garbage to the bodyguards of the prime minister, from pedophiles to State Department officials, and lately many of them have been telling her it's time for her to leave, if not for good, at least for a while. She stays here because this place opened a hole inside her. She doesn't know what's inside the hole, she just knows it hurts and the only way to respond is with love and compassion. This is her job, her real job. But tonight there's crying and yelling and a lot of expressed anger. She's my guide, the best. . . .

No Happy Endings

It comes to an end, for me, late at night in a discotheque, a hip place with murals of fantasy scenes from a tropical island. There's a dance floor with a mirror ball and strobe lights pulsing to Cambodian disco music, bodies crushed together, writhing like snakes in a pit. I'm sorry but I can't get into it. I stay in a booth and lie down, looking up and over at a glassed-off private room that's dark except for a television on the wall showing a *National Geographic* program on chimpanzees. There are five or six men in the room, customers, sitting in chairs, and four young women serving beer and walking around in high heels and very short skirts. Two men in suits guard the door. The men in the chairs look bored and tired, uninterested in the women, and there's a chimpanzee on the screen pounding, pounding, pounding a coconut or something like a coconut with a rock. I think it's a female chimpanzee, and it seems like she is pounding the rock just to show off to the other chimpanzees around her, as if it's her rock and she is pounding with it and none of the other chimps is going to stop her. She's happy, she has a tool and she knows how to use it.

I look to the dance floor and it is also pounding. Lisa is dancing with two Cambodian women, her friends, "professional girlfriends" who were both sold into prostitution before they reached puberty and now support their large families as paid mistresses to sad middle-aged Westerners. They are a success, in a way, but still call Lisa to borrow money when things get tight. Lisa's trying to dance with her friends, but it seems half the men on the floor, all Cambodian, have surrounded her. This bothers me (did I say I am in love with her?), but she's like, "okay, whatever." I look back to the *National Geographic* special and the chimp is still pounding. Enough, we get it—chimps know how to use tools. From the stone to the strobe light, pounding, pounding, pounding. I understand everything. I understand nothing. I close my eyes and try to sleep.

9

Economic Development Can End Slavery

Sam Saverance

Sam Saverance writes for The Graduate Voice.

History reveals that economics, not politics, is the key to under-standing modern-day slavery. This is why slavery has become such a large problem in many developing, poor nations such as Niger, Sudan, and Myanmar. While Western countries such as the United States also have a problem with slavery, the ratio of free persons to enslaved persons is much less significant than in Thailand or India. Because economics is key to understanding slavery today, it is also key to finding a solution. By combining economic development with democratic reform, slavery will eventually end as it becomes less profitable.

Slavery and economics go hand-in-hand. Slavery is synonymous with currency, machinery, and capital. Once more efficient means of currency, machinery, and capital are found, slavery becomes useless as an economic force. People don't hold slaves just to be "mean." It is greed that is the impetus for slavery, not evil. Greed is not something that we—as a political entity—can control; it will require much more vast social upheavals to overcome this basic human vice. The best we can do now is to provide a more humanitarian outlet for individual greed that is more beneficial to society than slavery is. This is accomplished through stratified economic growth and transparency.

Sam Saverance, "Slavery and Economic Development," *The Graduate Voice*, December 1, 2005. Reproduced by permission of the author.

To understand the relationship between economics and slavery, we only have to look at our past. History has shown that slavery rises and falls primarily on economic rather than political events. The British practiced slavery up until the Industrial Revolution in the late 18th century, after which the introduction of machinery and automation eliminated the need for slaves. In the pre-Civil War United States, the relationship between economics and slavery [is] most evident; the North was industrializing and finding more efficient ways to use its labor force, eliminating the need for holding slaves, while the South still relied on widespread agriculture and required vast amounts of manual labor to maintain its economy. The escalating conflict that resulted in the Civil War was as much a battle between two economic philosophies as it was a battle over slavery; it was not abolished on purely humanitarian grounds, but more on the argument that it was not an economically sound policy. Other nations such as Brazil continued to practice slavery up to the end of the 19th century, until industrialization rendered the institution unnecessary [in those places] as well.

Economic growth must go hand-in-hand with a democratic and balanced political system.

Slavery in Poor Nations

Today, most countries where slavery is a serious issue have poor, developing economies. The state of Mauritania, one of the poorest in the world, officially abolished slavery only 20 years ago and still has one of the most rampant trades in the world. It began over a thousand years ago when light-skinned Arabs and Berbers invaded the region and enslaved many of the darker-skinned inhabitants. Today, slavery has become an established tradition among Mauritanians, practiced by both light- and dark-skinned [people]. In a country where the average personal income is 1/50 that of a US citizen, and where subsistence agriculture is still the main source of income, a slave is a very valuable resource. . . . Take away that resource without substituting . . . something else [for it] and the economic effects can be very detrimental.

Countries where slavery is endemic are also countries that face serious development issues. In addition to Mauritania, poor countries like Niger, Sudan, and Myanmar are guilty of allowing slavery to flourish. This is not to say that developed countries do not have a slavery problem as well. Even in the US, there is serious concern over the number of people [who] enter the country as someone else's property. The greatest example of a relatively developed country with a human trafficking problem is Thailand, which has a thriving and brutal industry of trafficking young female prostitutes. However, in the example of the US, the numbers are not nearly as staggering as in poorer countries, with an estimated slavery rate of 1 in 3,000. Thailand's rate is higher, estimates ranging between 1 in 1,850 and 1 in 325, but it still is not as high as the 1 in 73 ratio in India and the staggering 1 in 6 rate in Myanmar. In Mauritania, estimates of enslaved people range from 100,000 to as many as 1 million, horrifying numbers in a country of only 3 million people. . . . There is a clear sliding scale between a country's economic prosperity and its rate of slavery.

An Economic Solution

While it seems appropriate to take an altruistic approach to ending the slavery problem, the sad fact is that it will not produce the desired results that an economic approach will provide. Again, we can look at the Civil War as an example. The South, upon losing the war, was immediately stripped of its resources, including slaves, and suffered a deep depression for many decades thereafter, affecting the freed slaves most severely. If slaves are to be freed, they must be so in favorable economic circumstances, because it is inevitable that they will begin their freedom on the lowest rung of the social ladder. In many cases, freed slaves are faced with conditions that are worse than when they were in bondage. An economic solution to slavery is the most beneficial way to ensure a smooth transition from slavery to citizenship, with a resulting standard of living that is at least manageable.

So what does an economic solution entail? There is a prominent argument being made that developed nations should "pay off" slaveholders in other nations to free their slaves. While this approach is extreme, it does make sense to provide an economic alternative to slavery for nations involved in the trade. The best method to reduce and eventually eradicate slavery in these countries is through transparent economic development—building industrialized, self-sufficient nations with the majority of workforces engaged in industry and commerce as opposed to agriculture. The growth and prosperity in India, should it continue with the proper transparency and distribution of wealth, will eventually lessen the need for mass labor in agriculture and lower the social barriers resulting from the caste system that relegate people to virtual slavery for life. However, economic growth must go hand-in-hand with a democratic and balanced political system. Myanmar may eventually achieve economic growth, but most of its slavery is enforced by a repressive military regime. This country and others such as North Korea and Cuba are exceptions to the rule, as state-instituted slavery supersedes any market-oriented slave trade. However, for the majority of nations facing slavery issues, the current course of economic development will eventually make slavery economically unfeasible.

Through the lessons of history, and an observation of the relationship between a nation's prosperity and [the] prominence of slavery, it is clear to see that economic growth is the most effective and attainable solution to the global slavery problem. The alternative—forcing countries to enforce slavery laws already on the code—is harmful to the economy and the emancipated slaves if the economic infrastructure is not present to support the freed citizens. While it seems cruel and inhuman to avoid the activist stance, [doing so] is the best way to get to accomplish the ultimate humanitarian goal.

10

Economic Development Causes Slavery

Justin Guay

Justin Guay is a graduate student at the University of Denver.

Modern-day slavery exists because of capitalism and free trade. Free trade has ruined traditional cultures and economies, leaving large populations poor and vulnerable. Slave traders have taken advantage of these populations; children, because of their vulnerability, have also become a common target for traders. Because of these factors, there are more slaves today than ever before in human history. To combat modern-day slavery, one must educate the public and address the economic underpinnings of the problem. International companies whose products are made by slave labor must be held accountable, while governments must curtail free trade's impact on developing nations around the world.

"Slavery existed before money or law" [Adam Hochschild, *Bury The Chains*, 2005]. Indeed the "peculiar institution" is one of humanity's oldest. It has, however, evolved and manifested itself quite distinctly in different periods of history. In contrast to historical views of slavery that are associated with chattel slavery, numerous forms fall under the umbrella term of contemporary slavery. The United Nations (U.N.) Working Group recognizes such radically new forms as: child labor, children in conflict, trafficking in persons, sexual exploitation, and the sale of children. The International

Justin Guay, "The Economic Foundations of Contemporary Slavery," *Human Rights & Human Welfare*. Reproduced by permission.

Labor Office (ILO) approaches the topic through the lens of forced labor. The ILO recognizes slavery and abductions, compulsory participation in public works projects, forced labor in agriculture, domestic workers, bonded labor, forced labor imposed by the military, forced labor in the trafficking of persons, as well as some aspects of prison labor and rehabilitation through work. A linking factor among these varied forms of contemporary slavery, according to the U.N. Working Group, is the role that poverty plays in creating vulnerability. This link is echoed in the work of Kevin Bales, arguably the world's foremost expert on contemporary slavery. According to Bales, contemporary slavery is "the complete control of a person, for economic exploitation, by violence, or the threat of violence." Using this definition, it is possible to explore the economic links that all forms of slavery, despite their unique characteristics, share.

Massive inequality and poverty have set the stage for the most profitable form of slave trading ever seen.

Economic conditions are decisive in the formation of slavery. Chattel slavery emerged as a disturbing manifestation of a push for labor-intensive goods created in the new world. Slaves were seen as property—as a form of investment. The ensuing ownership created a myriad of costs for slave traders and owners. These costs included cargo, shipment, and insurance during delivery, as well as the costs of maintaining the investment (food, medical treatment, and clothing) on behalf of the slave owner. Nearly forty million Africans lost their lives due to horrific conditions on slaving vessels. . . . Massive slave insurrections significantly added to the costs nations incurred in enforcing the trade. These economic realities, coupled with strong domestic opposition, eventually led slave traders and politicians in Great Britain to re-evaluate the desirability of the trade. This ultimately led to slavery's abolition in Great Britain and [subsequently] in ... countries around the world.

A new set of economic forces arose from the ashes of the Trans-Atlantic trade, as slave traders demonstrated their ability to adapt to a changing environment. During the post-abolition era, the colonial holdings of the world's imperial powers began to display an evolution towards slave-like practices. Forced labor by the state, debt bondage, and prison labor emerged to take the place of chattel slavery. These forms were markedly different for exactly what they lacked—namely, the immense costs and direct legal involvement in a trade that had been officially abolished. Imperial powers found these advantages to be economically and socially attractive. However, two devastating wars and the era of decolonization all but ended this period by the 1970s.

The vulnerability of the world's poor is a key ingredient to the successful implementation of ... [contract] slavery.

Capitalism, Free Trade, and Slavery

Economic factors have been shown to precipitate the rise and fall of different forms of slavery. The modern set of economic conditions, on which slavery now firmly rests, have arisen through the monolithic pillars of capitalism and free trade. Massive inequality and poverty have set the stage for the most profitable form of slave trading ever seen. Slaves today are, in purely economic terms, short term, low-capital investments with incredibly high rates of return. For example, slaves in the U.S. Antebellum South cost, in real terms, around $40,000; today, a slave goes for around $90. ... This is due to the enormous supply of slaves on the market today. In contrast to chattel slavery, ownership is now officially avoided. However, illegitimate contracts are used to keep victims in subjugation.

Although a dizzying array of slave-like practices [is] recognized, the dominating form of slavery today is debt bondage.

It is estimated that a staggering fifteen million of the world's slaves can be found in India, Nepal, Pakistan, and Bangladesh combined. . . . The primary method of enslavement in these countries is debt bondage. This involves a person using his or her labor as repayment for a loan. Unsavory accounting, astronomical interest rates, and violence then combine to keep the person in bondage that can last the rest of their life, and in many cases is passed on to generations of their descendants.

A common link in many forms of contemporary slavery is the use of illegal contracts. Domestic servants in the Philippines, textile workers in the United States, and sex workers in Thailand are all examples of contract slavery. The vulnerability of the world's poor is a key ingredient to the successful implementation of this type of slavery. Slave traders offer desperately poor people, usually in rural areas, employment through illegitimate contracts. Once the victim has been subjugated, the contract is used to keep the slave convinced that the arrangement is valid. The contract is also used to [sidestep] anti-slavery laws in case of problems with authorities. Despite the illegality of the practice, a lack of international enforcement allows the problem to persist.

Exploiting Children and the Poor

Perhaps most disturbing is the mass exploitation of children. According to the ILO, currently over 100 million children are being exploited for their labor. Children are especially attractive to slave traders because they are easy to coerce psychologically and physically. They are also valued for their small physical statures, which allow them to work in cramped conditions. The U.N., through the ILO, has committed itself to the abolition of the worst forms of child labor. These forms have been defined by the ILO as work, which by its nature, or the circumstances in which it is carried out, is likely to harm the health, safety, or morals of children. This work includes most forms of slavery or slave-like practices (the sale of a child, trafficking of children, bonded child labor, forced or compulsory labor including child soldiers), the commercial sexual exploitation of children (prostitution, pornography, forced child marriage, and child domestic work), and the use, procuring, or offering of a child for illicit activities (drug trade). . . .

The economic power wielded by the modern age slave holder is due to the seemingly unlimited supply of slaves in the world. According to the U.N., half of the world's six and a half billion people survive on less than two dollars per day. It is from this mass of desperately poor people that the world's slaves are culled. Never in history has there been a segment of society that is as vulnerable as today's poor.

The ideological push for the "science" of free trade has unleashed enormously destructive forces for social and cultural change that have wreaked havoc on the populations of developing countries. Rapid urbanization and restructuring of agricultural activities, upon which people have depended for centuries, has spelled disaster. In rural areas, the loss of common land combined with the switch to the production of cash crops from subsistence farming, has in effect destroyed people's livelihoods. . . . Heaped on top of this suffering is the destruction of the communities upon which people have depended for support.

Combating Slavery Today

As opposed to the later eighteenth and early nineteenth centuries, when slavery was confined to colonies and peripheral territorial holdings, contemporary slavery has permeated countries at every level of development in the global economy. Conservative estimates put the number of modern slaves alive today at 27 million. . . . Some human rights organizations have the number as high as 200 million. . . . This is more than all of the slaves who were captured and forced into slavery during the entirety of the Trans-Atlantic slave trade. The direct value of slave labor in today's economy is estimated between thirteen and twenty billion dollars. . . . It must be pointed out that these figures are strictly estimates. It is nearly impossible to discern any kind of verifiable, quantitative information on modern slavery, since slavery exists in the shadow of the global economy and thrives on the purposeful ignorance of states, multi-national corporations, and societies.

A market-based approach aimed at addressing the underlying factors involved must be implemented in order to combat the growing problem of contemporary slavery. Obscene profit, immense vulnerability, and lack of enforcement are the targets of such an approach. The supply and demand relationship is a good place to begin. Informing the public about goods that are produced by slaves will serve to reduce demand. On the supply side, multi-national corporations need to be held responsible for their labor practices and product sourcing. These objectives must be enforced by strictly adhering to existing laws on local, national, and international levels, thereby driving up the costs incurred by slave traders. Finally, governments and international organizations need to counterbalance the immense wealth disparity that is created by liberal economic policy. This can be achieved through economic policies aimed at human rather than economic development, including full employment and social welfare. This approach, aimed at reducing demand by developed countries, driving up the costs incurred by slave traders, and bringing up the income level of the majority of the world's poor, must be implemented globally in order to combat the ghastly effects that the slave trade has on humanity.

In order for us to end the reality of lives of servitude, which millions of people face today, and which millions more will face tomorrow, it is vital that we act now. The marriage of life and slavery may seem absolute, but it need not be. The future is defined by the actions of the present. In the words of Maya Angelou, "History, despite its wrenching pain, cannot be unlived, but if faced with courage, need not be lived again."

11

Slave Labor Exists in the United States' Agricultural Industry

Elias Lawless

Elias Lawless is a member of the Austin, Texas, affiliate of the Student/Farmworker Alliance.

Modern-day slavery may often seem like a problem that occurs somewhere else, but at the beginning of 2008, U.S. law enforcement officials discovered a tomato farm in Florida that used slave labor. These are the kind of abuses that organizations like the Coalition of Immokalee Workers (CIW) have been working to bring to an end. Unfortunately, it is difficult for governments to bring an end to slavery, primarily because corporations hold the balance of power in the world today. This simple fact has complicated the efforts of the CIW and other reformers: many corporations, while seldom directly involved in modern-day slavery, benefit from its practice. Tomatoes, for instance, are used at most fast food restaurants, meaning that familiar chains such as Taco Bell and Burger King have purchased agriculture products harvested by slave labor. Pressure can be brought to bear against these chains in a number of ways, the most effective being for people to quit buying their products. Through boycotts, fast food chains can be forced to demand that the growers who provide their produce respect human rights and fair wages.

Elias Lawless, "Petitioning the King: Ending Slavery and Sweatshops in Florida's Fields," *Dissident Voice*, March 31, 2008. Reproduced by permission of the author and *Dissident Voice*, www.dissidentvoice.org.

"Slavery, plain and simple." That's how Chief Assistant U.S. Attorney Doug Malloy described the most recent instance of forced labor uncovered in Florida agriculture.

An indictment released in January [2008], for a case still under prosecution, states that as recently as late November [2007], crew leaders for a tomato operation in Immokalee, Florida, were holding a group of men against their will—chaining them down, beating them, and locking them within a U-haul truck. The accused face charges of indentured servitude and peonage.

The men were kept on a property five blocks from the office of the Coalition of Immokalee Workers (CIW), a dynamic farmworker organization that won the 2007 Anti-Slavery Award, given by London-based Anti-Slavery International, the oldest human rights organization in the world.

The CIW has [assisted federal officials, uncovered, and investigated] in the successful prosecution of six slavery cases over the last decade—involving upwards of 1,000 people held against their will. And this case may soon be the seventh.

The impossibility of simply legislating an end to the practice of enslavement is all the more evident when we consider modern corporate power.

The CIW is doubtlessly best known, however, for forcing McDonald's and Yum Brands—the planet's largest fast food chain and restaurant company, respectively—to confront human rights abuses in the fields where they buy their tomatoes.

And so while 2008 marks the (curiously uncommemorated) bicentennial of social movements triggering the U.S. ban on the importation of enslaved Africans, slavery clearly continues to thrive.

Why Does Slavery Still Flourish

The impossibility of simply legislating an end to the practice of enslavement is all the more evident when we consider modern corporate power: we live in an era where the majority of the world's 100 largest economies are corporations, not governments.

Corporate influence is unquestionably prominent in our lives. Large, profit-seeking amalgams of capitalists exert unprecedented control over our daily experience—from the quality of the water we drink and the air we breathe, to our access to affordable and livable housing, and the way in which our food is produced.

While the CIW focused attention primarily on tomato growers as a solution to the violence and poverty they faced in the 1990s, their targets today are the major multinational corporations that buy massive volumes of tomatoes. After all, these corporations are profiting more than anyone from the reprehensible conditions in Florida's fields, including—in the most odious expression of the tomato industry's everyday exploitation—human enslavement.

An Oxfam Report dated March 2004, "Like Machines in the Fields: Workers Without Rights in American Agriculture," documents that while growers netted 41% of the retail price of tomatoes in 1990, by 2000 they were barely receiving one quarter. By purchasing huge quantities of tomatoes, fast food and grocery corporations wield tremendous power over small and large growers alike.

Growers cannot prevent the rising costs of gas, tractors, fertilizers, and so on; the one place they can control expenses is in how much they pay tomato pickers. Accordingly, due to the squeeze imposed on growers by multinational food corporations, tomato pickers' wages have remained essentially stagnant for 30 years, despite inflation.

The Slow Pace of Change

Precisely one year after the Oxfam report's release, and three years after a CIW-led boycott, Taco Bell conceded to CIW demands for higher wages and a supplier code of conduct. Never in the history of capitalism had a multinational corporation agreed to pay extra money down its supply chain to directly address the sub-poverty wages of workers at the opposite end.

The Taco Bell precedent tolled for the entire fast food and restaurant industry: a diverse movement of people of faith, workers, students, and community groups urged McDonalds to the table last April [in 2007], prompting even further-reaching accords. Yum Brands (parent company of Pizza Hut, Long John Silvers, KFC & Taco Bell) signed up all their companies shortly thereafter.

Thrillingly perched at the threshold of a more modern, more humane agricultural industry, the CIW looked to Florida-based neighbor Burger King.

Until recently, corporate rule has enjoyed unilateral communication about how they run things, with billions spent on advertising to shape how we think of their products and agenda.

But rather than partner with the CIW, whom FBI Director Robert Mueller mailed a letter of appreciation for their crucial role in the prosecution of multiple slavery cases, Burger King opted to instead join with the leaders of the industry that has generated federal convictions for forced labor, time and time again.

The Florida Tomato Growers Exchange—representing 90% of the state's tomato growers—has temporarily halted the groundbreaking penny-per-pound wage increase by threatening fines of $100,000 per offense, for any grower that participates, according to an Associated Press exposé.

Petitioning the King

Until recently, corporate rule has enjoyed unilateral communication about how they run things, with billions spent on advertising to shape how we think of their products and agenda. While people have protested governments for several centuries now, having learned to manifest outrage in a way that impacts destructive state policies, we stand in the incipient stages of discovering how to employ our collective voice in requiring the same accountability of today's for-profit sovereigns.

The CIW recently launched a major petition drive to end modern-day slavery and sweatshops in Florida's fields. While petitions may appear on the surface as a yawn-inducing riposte to injustice, the CIW's campaign echoes a key strategy employed by abolitionist forebears in England who used signature gathering to smash the slave trade there two centuries back.

Just as Burger King—among other fast food and grocery corporations—extracts extraordinary profit from the status quo of horrific labor conditions in Florida agriculture, British Parliament in the 1700s refused to end the slave trade due to the benefits they reaped from the plantation system: tremendous wealth from exploited labor.

While the state may not recognize the voices of these millions of people in their elections, conversely, fast food chains cannot afford to ignore them.

It was a petition campaign, exposing the overwhelmingly popular rejection of the cruelty of slavery, that compelled British decision makers to end it—an unauthorized people's referendum.

The British abolitionists, in their petition demanding an end to the slave trade, obtained signatures from more people than were actually eligible to vote for Parliament. Similarly, millions of people in the United States—including those convicted of felonies, those under the age of 18, and those who are not citizens—cannot lawfully vote for political office, but they can and do purchase hamburgers.

Ending Modern-Day Slavery

While the state may not recognize the voices of these millions of people in their elections, conversely, fast food chains cannot afford to ignore them. Accordingly, the CIW's petition campaign not only reflects a radically democratic means of incorporating all those who wish to make their voices count, it is also incredibly powerful because Burger King's constituents are, in fact, their would-be consumers.

The CIW petition demands that Burger King and other industry leaders:

- improve the wages and working conditions of the men and women who harvest their tomatoes, and

- support an industry-wide effort to end human rights violations and modem-day slavery in all of Florida's fields.

Beyond a declaration of support for the demands, the petition serves as an official registry of individuals pledging to boycott when CIW gives the word, stating that those who sign are "prepared to stop patronizing Burger King now, and other food industry leaders in the future, should they fail to [heed the demands]. . ."

In the words of CIW member Leonel Perez, "Slavery is not a problem without a solution." Indeed, two centuries after initial steps to abolish forced labor in US agriculture, it has become painfully obvious that passing more laws to further criminalize slavery will not end its practice—instead, we must develop an effective strategy to demolish the possibility that Burger King and others can continue profiting from the atrocious conditions that enable slavery to flourish.

12

Prison Labor Is State-Funded Slavery

Chris Levister

Chris Levister is a writer for New America Media.

It may surprise many to learn that a number of well-known clothing lines are being made by prison labor. Prison labor, in fact, has become a large growth industry, allowing corporations easy access to cheap workers. There are many questions, however, about human rights and prison labor. Employees are paid as little as 21 cents per hour for their labor and have little recourse if they are mistreated. The use of prison labor is also reminiscent of the historical practice in the American South of maintaining work farms where the labor of African American inmates was sold to contractors. Despite these problems, the prison industry continues to grow and is popular with inmates who are able to earn money and learn new job skills.

If you think prison inmates only make license plates, you're behind the times.

As a child Ayana Cole dreamed of becoming a world-class fashion designer. Today she is among hundreds of inmates crowded in an Oregon prison factory cranking out designer jeans. For her labor she is paid 45 cents an hour. At a chic Beverly Hills boutique some of the beaded creations carry a $350 price tag. In fact the jeans labeled "Prison Blues"—proved so popular last year [2005] that prison factories couldn't keep up with demand.

Chris Levister, "A Sweatshop Behind Bars," *WireTap*, September 13, 2006. Reproduced by permission.

At a San Diego private-run prison factory Donovan Thomas earns 21 cents an hour manufacturing office equipment used in some of LA's plushest office towers. In Chino Gary's prison-sewn T-shirts are a fashion hit.

Hundreds of prison generated products end up attached to trendy and nationally known labels like No Fear, Lee Jeans, Trinidad Tees, and other well known U.S. companies. After deductions, many prisoners like Cole and Thomas earn about $60 for an entire month of nine-hour days. In short, hiring out prisoners has become big business. And it's booming.

For the tycoons who have invested in the prison industry, it has been like finding a pot of gold.

The Prison Industry

At CMT Blues, housed at the Maximum Security Richard J. Donovan State Correctional Facility outside San Diego, the highly prized jobs pay minimum wage. Less than half goes into the inmates' pockets. The rest is siphoned off to reimburse the state for the cost of their incarceration and to a victim restitution fund.

The California Department of Corrections and CMT Blues owner Pierre Sleiman say they are providing inmates with job skills, a work ethic and income. In addition, he says prisoners offer the ultimate in a flexible and dependable work force. "If I lay them off for a week," said Sleiman, referring to his workers, "I don't have to worry about someone else coming and saying, 'Come work for me.'"

For the tycoons who have invested in the prison industry, it has been like finding a pot of gold. They don't have to worry about strikes or paying unemployment, health or worker's comp[ensation] insurance, vacation or comp time. All of their workers are full time, and [these workers] never arrive late or are absent because of family problems; moreover, if prisoners refuse to work, they are moved to disciplinary housing and lose canteen privileges. Most importantly, they lose "good time" credit that reduces [a prisoner's] sentence.

Today, there are over 2 million people incarcerated in the U.S., more than [in] any other industrialized country. They are disproportionately African-American and Latino. The nation's prison industry now employs nearly three quarters of a million people, more than any Fortune 500 corporation other than General Motors. Mushrooming construction has turned the industry into the main employer in scores of depressed cities and towns. A host of firms [is] profiting from private prisons, prison labor and services like transportation, farming and manufacturing.

Prison Labor and Human Rights

Critics argue that inmate labor is both a potential human rights abuse and a threat to workers outside prison walls, claiming inmates have no bargaining power, are easily exploited, and once released are frequently barred from gainful employment because of a felony conviction.

In one California lawsuit, for example, two prisoners have sued both their employer and the prison, saying they were put in solitary confinement after refusing to labor in unsafe working conditions. In a nutshell John Fleckner of Operation Prison Reform labels the growing trend "capitalist punishment—slavery re-envisioned."

Prison analysts say contract prison labor is poised to become one of America's most important growth industries.

The prison industry is not a new phenomenon, writes Fleckner. He says mixing the profit motive with punishment only invites abuse reminiscent of one of the ugliest chapters in U.S. history. "Under a regime where more bodies equal more profits prisons take one big step closer to their historical ancestor, the slave pen."

In fact, prison labor has its roots in slavery. Following Reconstruction, former Confederate Democrats instituted "convict leasing." Black inmates, mostly freed slaves convicted of petty theft, were rented out to do everything from picking cotton to building railroads. In Mississippi, a huge farm resembling a slave plantation replaced convict leasing. The infamous Parchman Farm was not closed until 1972, when inmates brought suit against [its] abusive conditions in federal court.

Prison Labor as a Growth Industry

Prison analysts say contract prison labor is poised to become one of America's most important growth industries. Many of these prisoners are serving time for non-violent crimes. With the use of tough-on-crime mandatory sentencing laws, the prison population is bursting at the seams. Some experts believe that the number of people locked up in the U.S. could double in the next 10 years. According to Prison Watch, the expansion of the number of prisoners will not only increase the pool of prison labor available for commercial profit, but also will help pay the costs of incarceration.

"The main goal of prison work programs is to provide a positive outlet to help inmates productively use their time and energies. Another goal is to instill good work habits, including appropriate job behavior and time management," according to the Joint Venture Program of the California Department of Corrections. The program is responsible for contracting out convict labor to governments, businesses and non-profit organizations.

Federal law prohibits domestic commerce in prison-made goods unless inmates are paid "prevailing wages" but because the law doesn't apply to exports, prison officials routinely market to foreign customers.

In California the prisons themselves are their own best customers. The California Department of Corrections purchases about half of what the prisons make, choosing from an online Prison Industry Authority catalog.

Low Wages, Popular Jobs

Prisoners now manufacture everything from blue jeans, to auto parts, to electronics and furniture. Honda has paid inmates $2 an hour for doing the same work an auto worker would get paid $20 to $30 an hour to do. Konica has used prisoners to repair copiers for less than 50 cents an hour. Toys 'R' US once used prisoners to restock shelves, and Microsoft to pack and ship software. Clothing made in California and Oregon prisons competes so successfully with apparel made in Latin America and Asia that it is exported to other countries.

In most states prisoners receive little of the money they earn working either for state-run or private sector corrections firms such as the Corrections Corporations of America (CCA) and Wackenhut. The labor prisoners perform is often considerably cheaper than in the outside world. Case in point, Texas-based Lockhart Technologies closed its Austin plant and fired some 150 workers who constructed circuit boards because it could relocate those jobs to a Wackenhut-run prison where detainees did the work for minimum wage.

But even with the low pay and potential for abuse, the labor programs are popular with prisoners, says California Prison Watch, which monitors the state's prisons. "Prisoner idle time is less, they earn spending money, and they can pick up a skill."

Tony Matos, 45, convicted of robbing a Rialto liquor store says, "When we step through the gates and into the shop, it's another world. This is a company. This isn't prison. Guards still keep watch, the capitalists still profit—the critics and supporters still debate. But in the end, I get a skill, a few coins, and a ray of hope and dignity."

13

Reparations for Slavery No Longer Has Public Support

Walter Olson

Walter Olson is a senior fellow at the Manhattan Institute and author of The Rule of Lawyers.

Beginning in the 1960s, a number of people believed that African Americans should receive reparations because of slavery. While the movement for reparations proceeded in stops and starts through the 1980s, it seemed to gain momentum in 2000 as it focused on the possibilities of lawsuits. This momentum, however, came to an end after the attacks on the World Trade Center in 2001. At that juncture, the very idea of reparations seemed to run counter to the mood of national unity. Furthermore, polls revealed that few people supported the idea. The one significant court case focusing on reparations following 9/11 failed, seeming to spell the end of the reparations movement.

Just a few years ago, at roughly the turn of the millennium [2000–2001], slavery reparations seemed the coming thing. A *New York Times* article in June 2001 reported that the movement to obtain compensation for slaves' descendants had "taken on substantial force" and was "gaining steam" both in the nation's universities and in the black community.

All the major black organizations had signed on, including the NAACP [National Association for the Advancement of Colored People], the Urban League and the Southern Chris-

Walter Olson, "Slavery Reparations: What Happened?" *Los Angeles Times*, October 31, 2008. Reproduced by permission.

tian Leadership Conference. Randall Robinson's book *The Debt: What America Owes to Blacks* had hit the bestseller lists in 2000. Many state and local Democratic politicians started to talk up the idea.

Then: nothing. Today, reparations seem to have completely disappeared from the national agenda. Few mention them anymore. What happened?

The Idea of Reparations

The idea of reparations for blacks had briefly come up at the time of the Civil War and the Emancipation Proclamation, but then was largely forgotten until 1969, when black militants, led by James Forman, began demanding a down payment of $500 million on future reparations. The brouhaha inspired liberal Yale law professor Boris Bittker to write *The Case for Black Reparations*, a book that appeared in 1973 and remains well worth a look 35 years later.

Bittker examined closely, but in the end dismissed as unpromising, the idea of filing lawsuits over blacks' past maltreatment. For Bittker, it made sense to pursue reparations not through litigation but through legislation funded from government revenues. And in the years that followed, the U.S. did just that, in a way, by vastly increasing spending on social welfare, education, housing and urban programs, aimed primarily at relieving black poverty, as well as taking explicitly compensatory and race-based steps in the schools and workplace— though these were not specifically designated as reparations.

The attacks of Sept. 11, 2001, broke this momentum [for reparations] with an abrupt jolt.

The movement reemerged in the late 1980s. This time, its advocates came mostly from law schools and embraced what Bittker had once ruled out: lawsuits against private parties. They sought to establish links between slavery and private actors not widely regarded as tainted by it—the more respectable, forward-minded and non-Southern these institutions, the better.

The polls made it clear too that a substantial sector of black opinion quietly opposed reparations as well.

Thus it came to light that some New England insurance companies in antebellum days had collected premiums from slaveholders for policies written on slaves' lives, and elite universities such as Harvard and Brown had received major financial benefactions from slaveholders and traders. As revelations of this kind emerged, a number of businesses and universities issued apologies or pledged increased donations to black causes.

Losing Momentum for Reparations

In late 2000, a new project called the Reparations Assessment Group began making preparations for lawsuits. The dollar sums mentioned were staggering. *Harper's* magazine estimated that it could require $97 trillion to pay for the hours of uncompensated work done during the slavery era, which would require extracting, on average, about $300,000 from every American of non-slave descent. So confident were reparationists of success that they began to map out how the court-ordered funds would be spent.

The attacks of Sept. 11, 2001, broke this momentum with an abrupt jolt. It wasn't just that for quite a few months thereafter Americans of all races preferred to discuss issues unrelated to reparations; it was also that some of the persistent themes that ran through those days, such as national unity, individual heroism, mutual dependence and the implications of mortality were at cross-purposes with the reparations narrative. According to LexisNexis, U.S. newspapers and wire services ran nearly 2,600 stories including the words "slavery" and "reparations" in the year leading up to 9/11. Since then, the yearly average has been less than 1,000.

But that was only part of what stopped the movement. The fact is, the hoped-for mobilization of public opinion had hit a wall. Editorialists and liberal churchmen aside, only a very small share of whites supported the idea—5% in one poll, 4% in another—while those opposed routinely topped 90%. The polls made it clear too that a substantial sector of black opinion quietly opposed reparations as well—and sometimes vocally, as when author Juan Williams slammed it as "a dangerous, evil idea [that could] take American race relations on a crash course."

The issue did resurface briefly in the media in the spring of 2002, with the filing of a class-action reparations suit that demanded $1.4 trillion from eight major corporations, including Aetna, Bank of America and the railroad concern CSX. Reparations lawyer Deadria Farmer-Paellmann and another freelancer, Richard Barber, had filed it, reportedly having grown impatient with the failure of the Reparations Assessment Group to act.

Dismissing Reparations

As a legal matter, the reparations claims proved desperately weak.

Consider the seemingly precedential claims arising from atrocities in wartime Europe. These suits did have several crucial advantages over slavery claims, most obviously that they arose from mistreatment of persons still or recently alive. Yet they mostly went nowhere before actual judges.

In 2005, a federal judge tossed out the Farmer-Paellmann and related reparations suits, in a decision largely upheld by the U.S. 7th Circuit Court of Appeals the next year [in 2006]. For most newspapers, the suit's dismissal was a back-pages story; everyone had moved on. To the extent the reparations movement had used its brief time onstage to encourage na-

tional introspection, Americans had reached a different con-
clusion from the one that the activists had hoped for—a rough
consensus, in fact, that whatever the right approach to the
nation's perennial problem of race relations might be, ven-
tures into anger-mongering and random expropriation weren't
it.

14

Reparations for Past Injustices Is an Ethical Issue

Donald W. Shriver, Jr.

Donald W. Shriver, Jr., is president emeritus of Union Theological Seminary in New York.

In recent years, a number of states have apologized for the institution of slavery, but an apology is only one part of our obligation to the past. Slavery may be in America's past, but its legacy continues to have a lingering impact on the lives of many African Americans. Living in poverty, many African Americans have fewer educational opportunities than other Americans, while a disproportionate number of African American men are incarcerated. Only by investing in education, medical care, and rehabilitation programs can we hope to resolve many of slavery's lingering social problems.

Between January 2007 and March 2008, six state legislatures passed resolutions of apology for their states' involvement in America's original sin of slavery. Five were Southern—Virginia, Maryland, North Carolina, Alabama, and Florida. The sixth was New Jersey.

Why have these apologies come so late? For the five Southern states, the resolutions came only after the election of significant numbers of African Americans to state legislatures. In Alabama, for example, at the time of the 1965 Selma civil rights marches, there was not a single African American in the

Donald W. Shriver, Jr., "It's a Start: Apologies for Slavery Must Be Followed by Steps to Justice," *Sojourners Magazine*, vol. 37, no. 6, June 2008, p. 8. Copyright © 2008 *Sojourners*. Reproduced with permission from *Sojourners*. (800) 714-7474, www.sojo.net.

state assembly. Thanks in part to [1965's] voting rights bill, by 2007 African Americans made up 25 percent of the body's membership.

Some of the apologies' key words—regret, contrition, acknowledgment, repentance, apology, reconciliation, healing—are central to Christian traditions. No serious Christian can doubt that sin has to be confessed to be forgiven. Legislatures need to confess that their predecessors put the seal of legality on slavery.

An Obligation to the Past

But an apology is only one element of healing in any fractured human relationship. The collective sin of slavery cries out for signals of collective repentance. As Maryland State Sen. Nathaniel Exum put it, "Once we have come to that recognition [of slavery], maybe we will also recognize steps we need to do to get rid of the lingering effects of it on the people." In saying that, he was contradicting the often-made argument that an apology does not, in the explicit words of the Virginia resolution, "justify the imposition of new benefits or burdens"—that is, monetary reparations.

Getting rid of slavery's "lingering effects" is a matter many whites in America prefer to overlook. As one opponent of the Alabama resolution put it, "It's time to move forward." Yes, but not so fast: The chains of America's racist past still rattle in the lives of many descendants of those slaves.

To apologize for a wrong entails some obligation to seek repair of its effects. Over the past century, America has done some repairing. The country has in many ways finally become serious about civil rights, and has offered episodic government remedies of past job and educational discrimination. Affirmative action has been an active form of reparation, touching the realities of unequal opportunity.

But there is much left to repair. Consider the challenge of enabling young black men to graduate from high school and to enter college in proportions equivalent to [those] of whites. That alone could be an important focus of reparations.

The Continued Impact of Slavery

At the end of his life, Martin Luther King, Jr., identified poverty, along with war, as the great unaddressed example of injustice in America. Not by coincidence, he noted, were young African Americans getting drafted to fight in Vietnam in numbers twice the proportion of blacks in the national population. As "employment opportunity" for the poor, war is a bad deal. Much better would be a program of public works, job training, and education for that most neglected category of residents in our urban areas: the half of young black men who do not finish high school.

Of the 1.5 million U.S. citizens in state and federal prison—a scandalously high number—about 38 percent are African Americans, most of them young. One in nine black males between the ages of 20 and 34 is behind bars, compared to one in thirty for the general population. Start putting as much money into education, medical care, and recovery from drug addiction as we put into building new prisons, and many of the lingering effects of our racist past might be tangibly addressed.

Public apology may be the beginning of telling the story and repairing the damage, but it should not be the end.

Perhaps the example of the states' apologies for slavery may encourage the U.S. Congress to follow suit. There, Rep. John Conyers' resolution H.R. 40—so numbered in memory of that body's failure to deliver "forty acres and a mule" to emancipated slaves—has been stuck in committee for almost 20 years. The resolution calls for a commission to study slavery and subsequent racial and economic discrimination against freed slaves, as well as the impact on African Americans today and possible remedies. Conyers' proposal is modeled on the commission Congress set up in 1980 to study the injustices done to Japanese Americans in the infamous internment camps during World War II. Eventually, each camp survivor was awarded $20,000.

Like Randall Robinson, author of *The Debt: What America Owes to Blacks*, Conyers wants the question of reparations to be discussed and thought about among Americans—all of them. Public apology may be the beginning of telling the story and repairing the damage, but it should not be the end.

15

Slavery Must Be Abolished Again

Mark P. Lagon

Mark P. Lagon was ambassador-at-large and director of the Office to Monitor and Combat Trafficking in Persons at the U.S. Department of State. In February 2009, he became executive director of Polaris Project, a Washington, D.C.–based anti-trafficking NGO (nongovernmental agency).

Mark P. Lagon, speaking from his experience in the key U.S. government position founded to combat modern slavery, defines human trafficking as "the slavery of our time." Lagon discusses debt bondage, sexual exploitation, forced labor, international trafficking and offender countries, U.S. involvement in human trafficking, and what can be done to combat and triumph again over this multifaceted modern slavery. Lagon speaks of the need for the United States to set an example of deep commitment to confronting trafficking within and across its borders in order to "elicit cooperation from other nations in eradicating human trafficking." Lagon uses human dignity as the guiding principle for formulating measures to help people suffering from human trafficking, and he calls for legal tools based on the principle of human dignity to "end the enslavement of some of the world's migrants." This essay incorporates some material delivered in the William V. O'Brien Lecture in International Law and Morality at Georgetown University on April 19, 2008, and a speech before the American Society for International Law on May 7, 2008 in Washington, DC.

Human trafficking is the slavery of our time. Exactly 200 years ago, Britain and the United States formally outlawed the transatlantic slave trade. A few decades later the practice of slavery was expunged from North America (with a heavy dose of justice enforced by the British Navy and of bloodshed in the American Civil War). While much has changed since the days of the transatlantic slave trade, the lie which fueled that horrific chapter in history is at the root of sex trafficking and slave labor today—a belief that some people are less than human.

Consider Carlo, a 27-year-old man from a rural area of the Philippines, recruited along with ten other men and women for a highly valued job in an American Midwestern hotel. The men were promised higher wages, reasonable hours, and benefits. Filipino recruiters charged each worker $1,200 as a "processing fee" for securing the jobs. Hotel mangers added new non-negotiable charges for "rent." This debt was used to coerce Carlo and the others to work endless hours.

Carlo's passport was confiscated by the traffickers to keep him from fleeing, which also rendered him undocumented and subject to potential arrest and deportation if caught by immigration officials off hotel premises. Toiling for 16 to 18 hours a day, Carlo and the other Filipinos endured total control by hotel managers over every aspect of their lives—what they ate, where they lived, and the hours they worked.

Debt Bondage

Carlo's story includes several threads which I increasingly see in my work at the State Department's Office to Monitor and Combat Trafficking in Persons. Carlo is a migrant. His nightmare began at the hands of a recruiter who used fraudulent offers of employment and extracted a large recruitment fee which Carlo could only pay by taking a loan. Carlo was uniquely vulnerable to exploitation once in the destination country, the U.S., due to the debt he carried as a direct result of recruitment. This home-country debt was exacerbated by fraudulent expenses, such as "rent," added by an exploitative U.S. employer.

Carlo's debt led to debt bondage. Lacking any form of power, not to mention identification, in a country not his own, Carlo was robbed of his dignity as a victim of forced labor.

Current trends fleshed out in the 2008 Trafficking in Persons (TIP) Report released by the Secretary of State in June, and produced by my office, paint a grim picture of the diffuse and diverse factors which contribute to the vulnerability of more than 175 million migrants in the world today—vulnerability not just to minor labor infractions but to gross exploitation.

The very factors that push migrants to leave their home countries are often the factors which make them vulnerable to the exploitation of trafficking when they arrive in a new destination.

Among these factors is the flagrant use of excessive debt as a tool of manipulation, the fraudulent practices of some middle-men brokering the movement of millions across international borders, weak laws—and weak enforcement of laws—governing labor exploitation, some aspects of sponsorship laws in Persian Gulf states, and a fundamental lack of understanding about human trafficking.

Debt bondage is a frequent form of forced labor. Too often, people are enticed into fraudulent offers of work abroad that require a steep payment up front for the services of a labor agency arranging the job or a payment that goes straight to the future employer. To pay such fees, workers in poorer counties either become indebted to the recruiter, or take out a formal or informal loan in their country of origin, with the expectation of payment based on future wages earned abroad.

Often, worker expectations and repayment terms are based on exaggerated and false representations by recruiters regarding wages the workers can expect to earn in their new jobs. Once at an overseas worksite, such high levels of indebtedness can make workers vulnerable to exploitation by unscrupulous employers who subject workers to terms much less favorable than promised at the time of recruitment (such as much longer hours, less pay, and harsher conditions).

The very factors that push migrants to leave their home countries are often the factors which make them vulnerable to the exploitation of trafficking when they arrive in a new destination. For example, millions of Burmese, facing bleak economic conditions, brutal political repression, and the prospect of forced labor at home, have fled homes and villages, usually without legal documents. The International Labor Organization (ILO) considers Burma to harbor a significant share of the estimated 2.2 million victims of state-imposed forced labor globally.

Burma's repression bleeds out into the surrounding region. As Harvard University professor Stanley Hoffmann wrote in *Duties Beyond Borders* in 1981—and it is every bit as true today—"There is no way of isolating oneself from the effects of gross violations abroad: they breed refugees, exiles and dissidents."(1) The grim situation in Burma serves to drive desperate people from their homes, often in irregular, undocumented migration.

Shortly after I became U.S. ambassador to combat human trafficking, I met Aye Aye Win—a young Burmese woman in search of work beyond her own tortured country. A recruiter painted a promising picture of work in neighboring Thailand. Aye Aye Win assumed substantial debt to cover upfront costs required by the recruiter for this job placement. Together with some 800 Burmese migrants, many of them children, Aye Aye Win was "placed" in a shrimp farming and processing factory. But it wasn't a job. It was a prison camp. The isolated ten-acre factory was surrounded by steel walls, 15 feet tall with barbed wire fencing, located in the middle of a coconut plantation far from roads. Workers weren't allowed to leave and were forbidden phone contact with anyone outside. They lived in rundown wooden huts, with hardly enough to eat.

Aye Aye Win tried to escape with two other women. But factory guards caught them and dragged them back to the camp. They were punished as an example to others, tied to poles in the middle of the courtyard, and refused food or water. Aye Aye Win told me how her now beautiful hair was shaved off as another form of punishment to stigmatize her. And she described how she was beaten for trying to flee. In countries where desperation leads people to migrate, it is easy for human traffickers and recruiters to market a dream, or a lie, to vulnerable men, women, and children like Aye Aye Win.

Dignity and Decency

It is important to clear up any misunderstanding about the differences between the issues of human trafficking and human smuggling or even illegal immigration—a charged topic in today's politics. Policies that conflate human trafficking and human smuggling or illegal immigration have the potential of punishing the very victims of trafficking whom we seek to protect. Human smuggling is the illicit transfer of some-one across sovereign borders, often with the consent of the person being smuggled. Human trafficking involves a defining element of gross exploitation and control over an individual.

As recognized in both U.S. law and relevant international instruments, human trafficking victims either do not consent to their situations, or, if they initially consent, later become victims of force, fraud, or coercion—like Carlo. The ongoing exploitation of trafficking victims generates illicit profits. Yet the sooner we understand that migrants who are victims of human trafficking are just that—victims—the sooner we will have a proper perspective, which looks beyond simply law enforcement mechanisms, for grappling with how to confront this challenge.

Part of that perspective must be informed by a basic understanding of the human dignity which should be accorded to all people under natural law. By "natural law" I mean the broad category of universal principles of dignity and decency which, while not law in and of themselves, have historically informed our understanding of basic human rights from the Declaration of Independence to the United Nations Universal Declaration on Human Rights. President George W. Bush and Secretary of State Condoleezza Rice have called these principles "the non-negotiable demands of human dignity." Natural law has proved to be a powerful force—one which moves history. It triumphed over slavery before and it can triumph again.

For these principles to triumph, we must fashion instruments to overcome the rapacious and the sadistic. Presently there are national laws and policy, bilateral accords, and international instruments available which we can employ in the service of human dignity to eliminate the vulnerability of migrants to trafficking.

International Trafficking

Among the most compelling tools at our disposal is the Protocol to Prevent, Suppress and Punish Trafficking in Persons, Especially Women and Children, supplementing the United Nations Convention against Transnational Organized Crime (a mouthful, but a worthy one). This protocol requires parties to criminalize all trafficking in persons, including trafficking for purposes of forced labor or sex.

In some regions of the world, particularly Asia and the Middle East, a number of governments have entered into bilateral agreements or Memoranda of Understanding (MOUS) in order to encourage and formally manage the flow of migrant workers from one country to another. To date, however, very few contain provisions explicitly protecting workers from conditions of forced labor or other forms of trafficking in persons. Even a country such as Saudi Arabia, with an estimated 7 million migrant workers imported largely for "3D" work (dirty, dangerous, and difficult), does not have sufficient protection for migrant workers.

We are encouraging labor-source and labor-destination governments in these regions to collaborate in confronting the problem of forced labor trafficking, including, when appropriate, through incorporation in bilateral agreements and Memoranda of Understanding specific measures to prevent trafficking in persons. Ironically, and tragically, some of those MOUS currently contain specific measures that promote trafficking, such as requiring the withholding of migrant workers' passports by employers in the destination country.

Labor-destination governments should consider steps to ensure that workers secured through third party recruiters are not the victims of fraudulent work offers or conditions of debt bondage.

Labor-source governments should: 1) Prohibit and punish labor recruiters who participate in trafficking by securing workers through fraudulent offers or imposing fees meant to create situations of debt bondage; 2) Ensure that labor recruiters are properly vetted, licensed, and monitored; and 3) Increase efforts to raise awareness of the trafficking risk associated with labor recruitment and migration.

Labor-destination governments should consider steps to ensure that workers secured through third party recruiters are not the victims of fraudulent work offers or conditions of debt bondage. The activities and practices of local labor brokers should be monitored, and such agencies, as well as employers, should be criminally accountable for acts of exploitation accomplished through force, fraud, or coercion against foreign workers.

All criminals responsible for human trafficking deserve potent penalties rather than suspended sentences or fines comparable to mere slaps on the wrist. Although there is still a massive lag in prosecution of forced labor trafficking versus sex trafficking cases, my office has noticed, in recent years, a rise in the number of reported cases of forced labor trafficking, some of which stem from otherwise legal transnational labor migration. But in many countries, there is official indifference in the face of labor trafficking, which is too often considered a civil, regulatory offense rather than a criminal act.

It is important that labor-destination governments encourage workers to report alleged cases of forced labor to law enforcement authorities and institute measures to ensure a worker can leave an abusive employer and seek legal redress without fear of automatic detention and deportation. Destination countries should take steps to make migrant workers aware of their rights. These efforts are invariably more effective where there are incentives for victims, such as provision of shelter, medical care, free legal aid with translation services, the ability to work while awaiting resolution of investigations, avenues for seeking restitution, and protection from possible retribution for having filed a complaint.

Finally, and perhaps most important, destination governments must ensure that exploitative employers and labor brokers are not allowed to abuse legal processes by having foreign workers who complain arrested, incarcerated, or deported. Workers who allege forced labor must have the opportunity to seek redress.

Migrants

Human trafficking is also a phenomenon occurring within national borders. In Brazil, for example, forced labor has typically involved young men drawn from the impoverished Northeast states—Maranhao, Piaui, Tocantins, Para, Goias, and Ceara—to work in the northern and central western regions of the county. Although the law prohibits forced or compulsory labor, including by children, forced labor and trafficking of workers has occurred in many states, most commonly in activities such as forest clearing, logging, charcoal production, raising livestock, and agriculture, particularly harvesting sugarcane, coffee, and cotton. The ILO estimated that there were approximately 25,000 forced labor workers in Brazil during the year 2007.

Labor intermediaries trafficked most forced laborers to remote estates, where victims were forced to work in harsh conditions until they repaid inflated debts related to the costs of travel, tools, clothing, or food. Armed guards sometimes were used to retain laborers, but the remoteness of the location, confiscation of documents, and threats of legal action or physical harm usually were sufficient to prevent laborers from fleeing.

In Brazil, while the central government has announced a national plan to combat trafficking in persons, violators of forced labor laws enjoyed virtual impunity from criminal prosecution, and no landowner has ever been convicted and imprisoned for using slave labor. In a positive step forward, the Ministry of Labor and Employment did punish those who used slave labor by imposing fines, requiring that indemnities be paid to the workers and placing the names of violators on a "dirty list," which was published every six months on the Internet.

Given the nature of forced labor trafficking, it is necessary for our efforts to expand beyond government action. The ILO, for example, is reaching out to the private sector and has developed a list of ten promising practices to help employers prevent forced labor in their own enterprises and cooperate with broader efforts to combat forced labor and trafficking.(2)

Goods enter the global marketplace while consumers have little or no knowledge of the supply chains and work conditions that resulted in their production. This is problematic for both the consumer and businesses which are increasingly faced with the challenge of ensuring that complex supply chains are untainted by forced labor.

Governments must protect victims of trafficking, including victims who are foreign migrants. For purposes of the annual U.S. Trafficking in Persons Report, one important component of victim protection considered is whether foreign victims of trafficking are provided with legal alternatives to deportation to countries where they face hardship or retribution. The United Nations Protocol on Trafficking in Persons also calls on state parties to consider offering victims of trafficking the ability to remain in their countries in appropriate cases.

North Koreans crossing the border with China are extremely vulnerable to trafficking given their illegal status in China and the harsh punishment they would face if they were to return home. Protection of victims should [be] the core principle of any effective anti-trafficking strategy. Greater government efforts need to be made to protect this highly vulnerable group.

At this time, China classifies North Korean refugees as "economic migrants" and forcibly returns some to the DPRK where, as noted, they may face severe punishment, including execution. The U.S. consistently urges China to treat North Korean asylum seekers in line with international agreements to which it is a signatory. The political sensitivity of this issue and a lack of transparency in China's law enforcement system have hampered our efforts to advocate effectively for change.

In many Persian Gulf states, which rely heavily on foreign migrant labor, individuals working as domestic servants, often migrant women, are particularly vulnerable to acute sexual and labor exploitation. They labor in lowpaying, poorly regulated sectors. In many such countries, to be a woman or a migrant often means less than equal treatment under the law and in practice. But to be a woman migrant leaves you in a particularly precarious position. So-called sponsorship laws—prevalent throughout the Gulf—have in practice been abused in too many cases by unscrupulous employers who require the migrant worker to do whatever they demand or else run the risk of deportation due to alleged breach of contract.

Less Than Human

Nowhere is this more evident than in Saudi Arabia, where every month, hundreds of female migrants, recruited as domestic workers, flee Saudi households in which they face severe abuse including rape, physical beatings, confinement, and denial of wages. The perpetrators of these trafficking crimes are Saudi husbands and wives who, as part of the Gulf's "maid culture," see foreign servants as less than human and acceptable for exploitation. Unfortunately, Saudi Arabia's criminal justice system too often validates this culture of abuse by failing to hold traffickers accountable. Reflecting an abject lack of political will to address this crime, Saudi Arabia has been on the TIP Report's lowest ranking for four years in a row.

Take Nour Miyati, an Indonesian woman who sought a brighter future for her nine-year-old daughter. Nour worked as a domestic servant for four years in the Saudi Kingdom. She was treated fairly and was able to send money back home so that her daughter could stay in school. Then her fate took a turn under a new employer, who confined her to his house, denied her pay, and tortured her. Injuries she suffered to her hands and feet resulted in gangrene that required the amputation of her fingers and toes.

Tragically, Nour was twice victimized. Despite having escaped these horrific circumstances, she was arrested for "running away" under the country's sponsorship laws and was not accorded proper status as a victim of trafficking. Workers such as Nour may escape abuse in private homes or work sites only to be denied an exit permit to leave the country.

As migration becomes increasingly feminized, more migrant women are at risk of being trafficked into prostitution.

Labor-destination countries should have procedures in place to ensure that foreign workers are screened for evidence of trafficking prior to being removed for lack of legal immigration status. Training law enforcement officials and immigration officers on victim identification, or the deployment of trained victim identification specialists, are among the measures destination countries should consider in order to improve their ability to identify trafficking victims.

The exploitation of domestic workers is not unique to the Gulf. The 2008 TIP Report highlights the case of two women—Mala and Kamala—who came to the U.S. to work as domestic servants for an American family on Long Island, New York. They accepted an offer of work in a far-away country in hopes of improving the livelihood to their families back in rural Indonesia. Instead, what they encountered in an affluent community of suburban New York City was a form of modern-day slavery. The two domestic workers were subjected to beatings, threats, and confinement until, after years, they sought help. Their exploiters were tried and convicted on multiple criminal charges, including forced labor and "document servitude" (withholding a person's travel documents as a means to induce them into labor or service).

Trafficking of migrant women is particularly relevant in the realm of commercial sexual exploitation. As migration becomes increasingly feminized, more migrant women are at risk of being trafficked into prostitution. Lila, a 19-year-old Romanian girl, who had already endured physical and sexual abuse from her alcoholic father, was introduced by an "acquaintance" to a man who offered her a job as a housekeeper or salesperson in the UK. When she arrived in the UK, the man sold her to a pimp, and Lila was pushed into prostitution. She was threatened that she would be sent home in pieces if she didn't follow every order. After an attempted escape, her papers were confiscated and the beatings became more frequent and brutal. Months later, after being re-trafficked several times, Lila was freed in a police raid. She was eventually repatriated back to Romania, where after two months she fled from a shelter where she had been staying. Her whereabouts are unknown.

Migrants are abused nearby, not just in far-off lands. Molina, a 30-year-old Mexican, was held against her will and forced to work in a factory in Southern California making dresses from 5:30 in the morning until 11 at night, seven days a week. She was not allowed to take a shower or leave the factory; at night she shared a small bed with another woman. She received one meal of beans and rice a day. If she didn't sew fast enough, her boss would pull her hair, pinch and slap her. The factory doors were locked during the day and at night a watchman prevented her from leaving. "If we wouldn't do what she [her boss] said, she told us somebody who we love would pay the consequences," says Molina.

Relief

To elicit cooperation from other nations in eradicating human trafficking, the U.S. needs to be seen as acknowledging that it confronts trafficking as well, as Molina's story illustrates, and that we are willing to share lessons learned as well as talk about areas where there is room for improvement. I work closely with domestic agencies to show other nations we are not just delivering diplomatic demands to others to change but are deeply committed to change ourselves. The U.S. government identifies our own areas for improvement in an annual self-assessment produced by the Department of Justice.(3)

Within the United States, the Trafficking Victims Protection Act of 2000 (TVPA), which created the office I direct, also created the "T" Visa which allows trafficking victims to remain in the United States to assist federal authorities in the investigation and prosecution of human trafficking cases, and to give them a place of refuge in the aftermath of severe exploitation. This status applies even to individuals who may have come here originally without proper documentation, if it is clear that they were victims of human trafficking.

From 2001 through January 2008, the U.S. Department of Homeland Security granted approximately 2,000 "T" visas to trafficking victims and their families, allowing them to remain in the United States. Human trafficking survivors from as many as 77 countries have been certified to receive certain U.S. federally-funded or administered benefits. Fortunately, Molina from the story above qualified for a "T" Visa under U.S. law and she now works as a security guard in Los Angeles; she's completed English classes and is working toward her GED.

The plight of exploited migrants, some of whom are susceptible to human trafficking, should not become enmeshed in our domestic immigration debate. We should be able to agree that those who arrive on our shores only to experience victimization in the form of human trafficking deserve proper care.

While this victim-centered approach is laudable and something that we encourage foreign governments to consider, there is still room to improve at home. Many trafficking victims do not know that this form of relief exists. Greater government efforts need to be made to educate a highly vulnerable group of victims regarding what protections are available. Otherwise, as in so many countries, victims hidden in the shadows of complex, insidious manipulation—what sociologist Kevin Bales calls "disposable people"(4)—are afraid to come forward and seek help, afraid to be treated as criminals and illegal aliens.

The plight of exploited migrants, some of whom are susceptible to human trafficking, should not become enmeshed in our domestic immigration debate. We should be able to agree that those who arrive on our shores only to experience victimization in the form of human trafficking deserve proper care. As a global leader, we encourage the same response abroad.

What to Do

In order to improve our awareness of forced labor abroad, and to discourage labor exploitation, the U.S. Department of Labor is currently developing a list of goods that the department has reason to believe are produced through forced labor or child labor in violation of international standards. The list, due in 2009, will serve as an awareness-raising tool for U.S. enforcement agencies, for the public, for governments, for NGOs, and ultimately for the business community. It is also consistent with U.S. government efforts to deny specific items produced, in part or wholly, by forced labor access to the U.S. market.

Amid the tremendous benefits that international migration brings, we cannot be blind to the dark side of the global economy—for it is in these shadows that trade in human beings is permitted to flourish. Whether it is an Indonesian migrant worker trapped in a factory in the Middle East, or an Eastern European girl prostituted and held captive in a brothel in Western Europe, or a young North Korean bride forcibly married to a Chinese man—these are the faces of modern-day slavery. They have become ensnared in human trafficking and forced labor and they demand our attention as they yearn for dignity.

Governments, both at the domestic level and through international cooperation, must work to improve protection for those migrants who are victims of trafficking while respecting their human rights—ensuring they are not treated as non-people. Most of these arrangements need not take the form of new treaties and multilateral institutions. As Anne-Marie Slaughter pointed out in [A] *New World Order*, "In this context, a world order based on government networks, working alongside and even in place of more traditional international institutions, holds great potential."(5)

To end the enslavement of some of the world's migrants, we need to focus on legal tools as well as other arrangements that further the fundamental principle of human dignity. This principle inspired Myres McDougal and Harold Lasswell, of the so-called New Haven school of legal thought, who wrote in 1959, "Our overriding aim is to clarify and aid in the implementation of a universal order of human dignity." To decrease migrants' vulnerabilities to human trafficking, we indeed need to focus on tools in public law (and also in less formal arrangements) which take into account the underlying concern of the New Haven school in advancing human dignity.

International cooperation can be achieved as well through the most prominent international instrument in this area, the UN Trafficking in Persons Protocol, a state-of-the-art UN instrument adopted in 2000, the same year that the U.S. Trafficking Victims Protection Act passed. The UN Protocol should be a touchstone, alongside ILO conventions and migration agreements, for confronting the special calamitous horror of human trafficking. More important than ratifying the protocol is implementing it. As important as enacting laws consonant with the protocol is vigorously enforcing them. Promoting human dignity is the common denominator in these arrangements, formal and informal, among or within nations designed to fulfill the natural law principle that fellow humans not be treated as less than human—as slaves. All governments, ours included, must embrace this obligation.

References

1. Stanley Hoffmann, *Duties Beyond Borders: On the Limits and Possibilities of Ethical International Politics* (Syracuse University Press, 1981), III.

2. International Labor Organization. Special Action Program to Combat Forced Labour (SAP-FL). http://www.ilo.org/sapfl/Events/ILOevents/lang--en/WCMS_092176/index.htm.

3. Attorney General's Annual Report to Congress and Assessment of the U.S. Government Activities to Combat Trafficking in Persons Fiscal Year 2007 (May 2008). http://www.usdoj.gov/ag/annualreports/tr2007/agreporthumantrafficing2007.pdf.

4. Kevin Bales, *Disposable People: New Slavery in the Global Economy* (University of California Press, 2000).

5. Anne-Marie Slaughter, [A] *New World Order* (Princeton University Press, 2005).

16

Religion Can Play a Role in Abolishing Slavery Today

Austin Choi-Fitzpatrick

Austin Choi-Fitzpatrick is the national outreach coordinator at Free the Slaves.

Modern-day slavery has become a public concern, and while the sheer enormity of the problem may make a resolution seem unlikely, such organizations as Free the Slaves are moving forward. In looking at the problem, however, one can also draw inspiration from the efforts of Christians to end slavery in an earlier period. Expanding on this legacy, a new abolition movement can be built from a broad variety of religious faiths. Together, Christians, Hindus, and many other people of faith can combine rich legacies of protest against injustice, and begin—as an interfaith alliance—advocating the creation of a slave-free world.

Slavery still exists. If you've been paying attention over the last few years, you'll have noticed this theme cropping up again and again. It started like a low rumble coming from human rights advocates, humanitarian workers, and missionaries the world over. A resurgence of a very, very old sort of exploitation was taking place among those least able to defend themselves. People at the margins of the economy, whether the global economy or their own village economy, were forced to do work with little or no pay and unable to leave because of violence and fear. That's what slavery is: forced work, no pay, and violence.

If you've been paying attention you've noticed that this issue takes an astounding number of forms: human trafficking, forced prostitution, bonded labor, forced marriage, forced conscription into armies . . . the list goes on, checked only by the limits of human imagination. These horrible things are happening to children, men, women—anyone caught in the fissures and gaps of an economy with nobody looking after them. And then there are the numbers: 27 million held in slavery worldwide, tens of thousands right here in the United States.

Glimpses of Hope

I've been working on this issue for years now and will be the first to admit that this steady stream of statistics and stories is bleak. But I've got to tell you about what else I've been seeing—something beyond slavery. Flashes of hope. Glimpses of freedom. I work for an organization called Free the Slaves. The more we learn the more we're convinced that complex problems require ambitious solutions. And these solutions must get us all thinking about slavery in terms of freedom.

In thinking about slavery and abolition, Christianity comes immediately to mind.

We recently released a book (*Ending Slavery: How We Free Today's Slaves*), written by sociologist and Free the Slaves president Kevin Bales, that sketches this ambitious solution. We believe it's going to take a mass movement of people standing up against slavery. People like you and me. It's also going to take governments enforcing their laws against slavery. And it will take corporations that have the courage to take a hard look at their supply chains, removing slavery wherever they find it. International groups like the UN [United Nations] and non-governmental organizations have a role too, building infrastructure for large-scale anti-slavery work. We think that together we can end slavery in twenty-five years. The book's most important contribution is that it opens a window into a world in which each of us has a role to play.

The Role of Faith Communities

So lately, I've been asking myself: What's the role of faith communities in all of this? My search for answers has broadened my horizons and gladdened my spirit. In thinking about slavery and abolition, Christianity comes immediately to mind. The relationship isn't a clean one. Many a theological battle was waged before the notion of freedom for the enslaved took root in Christian consciousness. In fact, broader ideas of freedom were slow to catch on, as lauded abolitionist William Wilberforce painfully displayed when he said that "taught by Christianity, [freed slaves] will sustain with patience the sufferings of their actual lot . . . [and] will soon be regarded as a grateful peasantry." . . .

And yet, there they were, Christians leading the last antislavery movement (and a few rebellions) some 200 years ago. In retrospect it may seem natural that the church would get involved in this effort. But it's important to remember what else the church was doing at the time. The church was also busy using the Scripture to defend slavery. The sociologist Christian Smith has pointed out that the "worldviews, moral systems, theodicies, and organizations of religion can serve not only to legitimate and preserve, but also to challenge and overturn social, political, and economic systems."

So who was doing the challenging and overturning? Who had the gumption to stand up against slavery when it was at its zenith? We must remember that the slave trade was one of the most significant industries in the global economy. It was backed by religious leaders and economic elites. And who stood up to say, "let's do away with a principal engine of the world economy because it's the right thing to do"?

It was people of faith. A handful with the courage to draw on the very best of their prophetic tradition and articulate a vision of freedom.

Abolitionist Movements

Sounds great! So who all's got this vision of freedom? Just Christians? The Buddhist tradition forbids the trading of weapons and people. Within Islam the Prophet Mohammed was fierce in his denunciation of slavery. His statement that "There are three categories of people against whom I shall myself be a plaintiff on the Day of Judgment. Of these three, one is he who enslaves a free man, then sells him and eats this money" echoes into the present. Within Hinduism a vibrant freedom movement is challenging the caste system and the slavery it supports. The Jewish faith has brought us one of the most significant narratives of emancipation: the Exodus of Jews out of enslavement.

What would a radically interfaith movement against modern slavery look like? What tools, traits, and traditions do[es] each of the world's religions bring to the table when it comes to this historic work?

In fact, abolitionist movements have been happening within religious movements for thousands of years. Wang Mang, the Buddhist Chinese Emperor, may have been the first powerful abolitionist. He outlawed the slave trade in [A.D. 9], some 2,000 years ago. Beginning in the eleventh century the Ismaili Muslim Druzes sect began criticizing slavery. They were also a leading voice in the call for abolition in the middle of the twentieth century. The nineteenth century reformer Sayyid Ahmad Khan has been called "the Islamic William Wilberforce." Hindu social workers, journalists, and doctors were at the forefront of the effort to end the practice of devadasi, or temple prostitution. In 2000 the Religious Action Center of

Reform Judaism signed a statement which reads: "Human trafficking destroys someone's spirit, displaces them from their community, and creates wounds that will never heal." The Free Methodists recently issued a declaration against slavery, their ninth since 1797. The Church of the Brethren's 2007 resolution states: "We confess our complicity in the global network of slavery through consumption of goods and services that have been produced by slave labor."

An Interfaith Abolition Movement

It is with these prophetic voices in mind that we can begin to ask ourselves: What would a radically interfaith movement against modern slavery look like? What tools, traits, and traditions do[es] each of the world's religions bring to the table when it comes to this historic work? Think about it: for thousands of years individuals and small groups of reformers have been asking themselves these questions about their own faith. Can you imagine the courage it took them to blend faith in action for the purpose of cultural transformation?

These are historic times, and a world free from slavery is within reach. This effort will only be successful when we work together from the best of our respective traditions, from the highest expressions of our faith.

I'm firmly convinced that this is exactly what we need—faith in action—an interfaith abolitionist movement linking people of all faiths together as they take action against slavery and for freedom. Sound unlikely? In fact, the struggle to end slavery has already resulted in unlikely alliances. Secular feminists have joined with stalwart evangelicals to pass landmark legislation on this issue. Both communities regularly contribute to the growing awareness that trafficking for sexual exploitation simply shouldn't exist.

What's needed now is unprecedented: an even broader movement of believers from all walks of life and from all faiths. These are historic times, and a world free from slavery is within reach. This effort will only be successful when we work together from the best of our respective traditions, from the highest expressions of our faith. Together we can ensure that our children live in a world free from slavery. So let's get started. Against slavery, for freedom. Today.

Organizations to Contact

The editors have compiled the following list of organizations concerned with the issues debated in this book. The descriptions are derived from materials provided by the organizations. All have publications or information available for interested readers. The list was compiled on the date of publication of the present volume; the information provided here may change. Be aware that many organizations take several weeks or longer to respond to inquiries, so allow as much time as possible.

Carnegie Council for Ethics in International Affairs
Merrill House, 170 East 64th Street
New York, NY   10065-7478
(212) 838-4120 • fax: (212) 752-2432
e-mail: info@cceia.org
Web site: www.cceia.org

The Carnegie Council is an international organization promoting ethical leadership on issues of war, peace, and global social justice. The Carnegie Council's mission is to be the voice for ethics in international policy. The council convenes agenda-setting forums and creates educational opportunities and information resources for a worldwide audience of teachers and students, journalists, international affairs professionals, and concerned citizens. The Council offers a broad array of reference material, including a quarterly journal titled *Ethics & International Affairs*, the *Insider*, and an electronic newsletter.

Center for Economic and Social Rights (CESR)
162 Montague Street, 3rd Floor, Brooklyn, NY   11201
(718) 237-9145 • fax: (718) 237-9147
e-mail: rights@cesr.org
Web site: www.cesr.org

The Center for Economic and Social Rights (CESR) was established in 1993 to pursue social justice through human rights. The CESR promotes economic and social rights as contained in the Universal Declaration of Human Rights. The organization protects the rights of all human beings to housing, education, health and a healthy environment, food, work, and an adequate standard of living. CESR publishes various articles, fact sheets, reports, and training materials.

Coalition for the International Criminal Court (CICC)
c/o WFM, 708 3rd Ave., 24th Floor, New York, NY   10017
(212) 687-2863 • fax: (212) 599-1332
e-mail: cicc@iccnow.org
Web site: www.iccnow.org

The Coalition for the International Criminal Court (CICC) is an international network of thousands of civil society organizations and hundreds of nongovernmental organizations (NGOs) dedicated to the establishment, acceptance, and implementation of the International Criminal Court. The CICC's objectives include: promoting awareness of the ICC and Rome Statute; facilitating the effective participation of civil society in the sessions of the Assembly of States Parties; promoting universal acceptance and ratification of/accession to the Rome Statute and the full implementation of the treaty's obligations into national law; monitoring and supporting the full establishment of the court; and promoting international support for the ICC. The CICC publishes numerous documents, including the magazine *The Monitor* and various newsletters and factsheets.

Amnesty International (AI)
5 Penn Plaza, 14th Floor, New York, NY   10001
(212) 807-8400 • fax: (212) 463-9193
e-mail: admin-us@aiusa.org
Web site: www.amnestyusa.org

Amnesty International (AI) is a worldwide movement of people who campaign for internationally recognized human rights. AI investigates and campaigns against human rights violations around the world. The organization undertakes research and actions focused on preventing and ending grave abuses of the rights to physical and mental integrity, freedom of conscience and expression, and freedom from discrimination. AI publishes a monthly magazine called *Wire* as well as numerous reports and documents about human rights around the world.

Captive Daughters

3500 Overland Ave., Suite 110–108
Los Angeles, CA   90034-5696
fax: (310) 815-9197
e-mail: mail@captivedaughters.org
Web site: www.captivedaughters.org

The mission of Captive Daughters is to end the sexual bondage of female adolescents and children. Its goal is to educate the public about the worldwide problem of sex trafficking and to promote policies and action to prevent such activity. Its Web site publishes an annotated bibliography of books, films, and previously published articles, including "Sex Trafficking: The Real Immigration Problem."

Coalition Against Trafficking in Women (CATW)

PO Box 7427, Jaf Station, New York, NY   10116
fax: (212) 643-9896
e-mail: info@catwinternational.org
Web site: www.catwinternational.org

The Coalition Against Trafficking in Women (CATW) is a nongovernmental organization that promotes women's human rights. It works internationally to combat sexual exploitation in all its forms, especially prostitution and trafficking in women and children. CATW publishes articles, reports, and speeches on issues related to sex trafficking, including "On the Battlefield of Women's Bodies: An Overview of the Harm of War to Women" and "The Case against the Legalization of Prostitution," which are available on its Web site.

Free the Slaves
1320 19th Street NW, Suite 600, Washington, DC   20036
(202) 775-7480 • fax: (202) 775-7485
e-mail: info@freetheslaves.net
Web site: www.freetheslaves.net

Free the Slaves is dedicated to ending slavery worldwide. It partners with grassroots anti-slavery organizations and concerned businesses to eradicate slavery from product supply chains and to build a consumer movement that chooses slave-free goods. Free the Slaves also encourages governments to draft and enforce effective anti-slavery and anti-trafficking laws. The organization publishes such reports as *International Trafficking in Women to the United States: A Contemporary Manifestation of Slavery and Organized Crime*, which is available on its Web site.

Global Rights
1200 Eighteenth Street NW, Suite 602
Washington, DC   20036
(202) 822-4600 • fax: (202) 822-4606
Web site: www.globalrights.org

Global Rights is a human rights advocacy group that partners with local activists worldwide to challenge injustice. The organization opposes U.S. laws that require organizations receiving U.S. global HIV/AIDS and anti-trafficking funds to adopt organization-wide positions opposing prostitution. Global Rights claims that such laws restrict the ability of local activists to prevent the spread of AIDS and to advocate for the health and human rights of women and men in prostitution. It publishes the quarterly magazine *Voices*, plus news, reports, and analysis on trafficking. Articles such as "Slavery in Our Midst: The Human Toll of Trafficking" are available on its Web site.

Human Rights Watch
350 Fifth Ave., 34th Floor, New York, NY   10118-3299
(212) 290-4700 • fax: (212) 736-1300

e-mail: hrwnyc@hrw.org
Web site: www.hrw.org

Founded in 1978, Human Rights Watch is a nongovernmental organization (NGO) that conducts systematic investigations of human rights abuses, including sex trafficking, in countries around the world. It publishes many books and reports on specific countries and issues, as well as annual reports, recent selections of which are available on its Web site.

International Justice Mission (IJM)
PO Box 58147, Washington, DC   20037-8147
(703) 465-5495 • fax: (703) 465-5499
e-mail: contact@ijm.org
Web site: www.ijm.org

The International Justice Mission (IJM) is a human rights agency that rescues victims of violence, sexual exploitation, slavery, and oppression. Its goals include rescuing victims, bringing accountability under the law to perpetrators, preventing future abuses, and helping victims transition to new lives. IJM publishes articles, reports, and books, including *Terrify No More*, which documents IJM's raids in the Cambodian village of Svay Pak, where its workers rescued thirty-seven underage victims of sex trafficking. The book can be purchased on its Web site for a small donation.

Polaris Project
PO Box 77892, Washington, DC   20013
(202) 745-1001 • fax: (202) 745-1119
e-mail: info@polarisproject.org
Web site: www.polarisproject.org

The Polaris Project is a multicultural grassroots organization that combats human trafficking and modern-day slavery. Based in the United States and Japan, it brings together community members, survivors, and professionals to fight trafficking and slavery. The project's goals include empowering trafficking survivors and effecting long-term social change to end trafficking.

United Nations Headquarters (UN)

First Avenue at 46th Street, New York, NY   10017
e-mail: inquiries2@un.org
Web sites of interest: www.un.org/Pubs/CyberSchoolBus/
humanrights/qna.htm; www.un.org/geninfo/faq; and www.un
.org/works

The United Nations (UN) is a vast organization comprising
more than 30 affiliated organizations and bodies that seek to
solve the myriad problems challenging humanity. The UN and
its family of organizations work to promote respect for human rights, protect the environment, fight disease, and reduce
poverty. UN agencies define the standards for safe and efficient air travel and help improve telecommunications and enhance consumer protection. The United Nations leads the international campaigns against drug trafficking and terrorism.
Throughout the world, the UN and its agencies assist refugees,
set up programs to clear landmines, help expand food production, and lead the fight against AIDS. With regard to human rights issues, the UN publishes such books and maga-
zines as the *UN Chronicle*, a quarterly publication that
provides in-depth coverage and information on the UN General Assembly, and *Africa Renewal*, which provides up-to-date
information and analysis of the major economic and development challenges facing Africa today.

United Nations Children's Fund (UNICEF)

UNICEF House, 3 United Nations Plaza
New York, NY   10017
(212) 326-7000 • fax: (212) 887-7465
e-mail: information@unicefusa.org
Web site: www.unicef.org

The United Nations Children's Fund (UNICEF) was created
(as the United Nations International Children's Emergency
Fund) on December 11, 1946. UNICEF provides long-term
humanitarian and developmental assistance to children and
mothers in developing countries. Guided by the Convention
on the Rights of the Child, the organization works to secure

the rights, survival, development, and protection of children worldwide. Each year UNICEF publishes *The State of the World's Children* and *Progress for Children*, as well as several other reports on children's human rights, such as *Africa's Orphaned and Vulnerable Children: Children Afflicted by AIDS* and *Pneumonia: The Forgotten Killer of Children*. UNICEF also publishes an electronic newsletter at least once each month.

U.S. Department of Labor

Bureau of International Labor Affairs (ILAB)
Washington, DC   20210
(202) 693-4770
Web site: www.dol.gov/ilab

The Bureau of International Labor Affairs (ILAB) carries out the U.S. Department of Labor's international responsibilities and assists in formulating the international economic, trade, and immigration policies that affect American workers. Its reports on child labor include the two-volume *By the Sweat and Toil of Children* and *The Apparel Industry and Codes of Conduct: A Solution to the International Child Labor Problem?*

Women's Refugee Commission

122 East Forty-Second Street, New York, NY   10168-1289
(212) 551-3088 • fax: (212) 551-3180
e-mail: info@womenscommission.org
Web site: www.womenscommission.org

The Women's Refugee Commission offers solutions and provides technical assistance to ensure that refugee women, children, and adolescents are protected and have access to education, health services, and livelihood opportunities. It makes recommendations to U.S. and United Nations policymakers and nongovernmental organizations (NGOs) on ways to improve assistance to refugee women and children. Experts conduct field research and technical training in refugee camps and detention centers. On its Web site, the commission publishes findings in its semi-annual newsletter, *Women's Commis-*

sion News, reports, and articles, including "The Struggle Between Migration Control and Victim Protection: The UK Approach to Human Trafficking."

Bibliography

Books

Kevin Bales	*Disposable People: New Slavery in the Global Economy.* Berkeley, CA: University of California, 2004.
Kevin Bales	*Ending Slavery: How We Free Today's Slaves.* Berkeley, CA: University of California, 2008.
Kevin Bales	*Understanding Global Slavery: A Reader.* Berkeley, CA: University of California, 2005.
Kevin Bales and Rebecca Cornell	*Slavery Today.* Berkeley, CA: Groundwood Books, 2008.
Kevin Bales and Zoe Trodd, editors	*To Plead Our Cause: Personal Stories by Today's Slaves.* New York: Cornell, 2008.
David Batstone	*Not for Sale: The Return of the Global Slave Trade—And How We Can Fight It.* New York: Harper One, 2007.
John Bowe	*Nobodies: Modern American Slave Labor and the Dark Side of the New Global Economy.* New York: Random House, 2008.
Anthony M. DeStefano	*The War on Human Trafficking: U.S. Policy Assessed.* Piscataway, NJ: Rutgers, 2007.

Kathryn Farr *Sex Trafficking: The Global Market in Women and Children.* New York: Worth, 2004.

Zach Hunter *Be the Change: Your Guide to Freeing Slaves and Changing the World.* Grand Rapids, MI: Zondervan, 2007.

Siddharth Kara *Sex Trafficking: Inside the Business of Modern Slavery.* New York: Columbia, 2008.

Gilbert King *Woman, Child for Sale: The New Slave Trade in the 21st Century.* New York: Chamberlain, 2004.

Victor Malarek *The Natashas: Inside the New Global Sex Trade.* New York: Arcade, 2005.

Craig McGill *Human Traffic: Sex, Slaves and Immigration.* London: Vision, 2003.

Jesse Sage and Liora Kasten, editors *Enslaved: True Stories of Modern-Day Slavery.* New York: Palgrave Macmillan, 2008.

E. Benjamin Skinner *A Crime So Monstrous: Face-to Face With Modern Slavery.* New York: Simon & Schuster 2008.

Sheldon X. Zhang *Smuggling and Trafficking in Human Beings: All Roads Lead to America.* Westport, CT: Praeger, 2007.

Periodicals

Kevin Bales and Steven Lize	"Investigating Human Trafficking: Challenges, Lessons Learned, and Best Practices," *FBI Law Enforcement Bulletin*, April 2007.
Rory Callinan	"Stolen Children," *Time International*, September 1, 2008.
Kevin Clarke	"Hidden in Plain Sight: The Shadow World of Human Trafficking," *U.S. Catholic*, December 25, 2008.
Mick Dumke	"Better Late Than Never? Some States Apologize for Their Role in Slavery," *Current Events*, April 23, 2007.
Mick Dumke	"Reparations Battles," *Chicago Reporter*, December 2003.
Hippolyte Fofack	"A Continued Abomination: Slavery in West Africa," *Economist (US)*, November 1, 2008.
Hippolyte Fofack	"The Incomplete Legacy of the Abolition of Slavery," *African Business*, April 2007.
Hippolyte Fofack	"Sea of Tears: People-Trafficking in Odessa," *Economist (US)*, September 23, 2006.
Sarah Garland	"This Woman Was Forced Into Slavery . . . in the U.S.," *Marie Claire*, May 2006.

Amardeep   "Today's Slavery: Understanding
Kaur Gill   Human Trafficking in the
Twenty-First Century," *Canadian Dimension*, May–June 2007.

Clare Goff   "Anti-Slavery Pioneers," *New Internationalist*, March 2007.

Viv Groskop   "Not For Sale," *New Statesman*, May 29, 2008.

Kimbriell Kelly   "Sold in the U.S.A.," *Chicago Reporter*, May–June 2006.

Melissa McNally   "Women Rebuild Lives after Horrors of Human Trafficking," *National Catholic Reporter*, August 31, 2007.

Brendan O'Neill   "The Myth of Trafficking," *New Statesman*, March 27, 2008.

Brendan O'Neill   "Sex Trafficking—The Facts: Trafficking for Sexual Exploitation Has Become An Epidemic in the Past Decade," *New International*, September 2007.

Kwesi Quartey   "Slavery: The Case for Reparations," *New African*, January and February 2008.

Dana Thomas   "The Fight against Fakes," *Harper's Bazaar*, January 2009.

Emma Thompson   "Behind the Door," *Newsweek International*, March 17, 2008.

Walter H. White   "Protecting and Advancing the International Rule of Law," *Human Rights*, Winter 2007.

Index